AMERICAN COOKBOOK

Discover Delicious American Recipes From All-over the United States

(Classical Comfort Foods From American Kitchens)

Dawn Smith

Published by Sharon Lohan

© **Dawn Smith**

All Rights Reserved

American Cookbook: Discover Delicious American Recipes From All-over the United States (Classical Comfort Foods From American Kitchens)

ISBN 978-1-7776245-2-1

All rights reserved. No part of this guide may be reproduced in any form without permission in writing from the publisher except in the case of brief quotations embodied in critical articles or reviews.

Legal & Disclaimer

The information contained in this book is not designed to replace or take the place of any form of medicine or professional medical advice. The information in this book has been provided for educational and entertainment purposes only.

The information contained in this book has been compiled from sources deemed reliable, and it is accurate to the best of the Author's knowledge; however, the Author cannot guarantee its accuracy and validity and cannot be held liable for any errors or omissions. Changes are periodically made to this book. You must consult your doctor or get professional medical advice before using any of the suggested remedies, techniques, or information in this book.

Table of contents

Part 1 1
Introduction 2
Alabama 3
Fried Green Tomatoes 3
Alaska 5
King Salmon Bake 5
Arizona 7
Chimichingas 7
Arkansas 10
Deep-Fried Catfish 10
California 12
Fish Tacos 12
Colorado 14
Colorado River Trout 14
Connecticut 16
New Haven Steamed White Clam Pizza 16
Delaware 19
Scrapple 19
Florida 21
Key Lime Pie 21
Georgia 23
Lattice Top Georgia Peach Pie 23
Hawaii 26
Ahi Poke 26
Idaho 28

Finger Steak	28
Illinois	31
Chicago-Style Deep-Dish Pizza	31
Indiana	35
Breaded Pork Tenderloin Sandwich	35
Iowa	38
Loose Meat Sandwich	38
Kansas	40
Kansas-City-Style Ribs	40
Kentucky	43
Kentucky Fried Chicken	43
Louisiana	46
Jambalaya	46
Maine	49
Lobster Rolls	49
Maryland	51
Crab Cakes	51
Massachusetts	54
New England Clam Chowder	54
Michigan	57
Michigan Cherry Pie	57
Minnesota	60
Minnesota Hot Dish	60
Mississippi	62
Mississippi Mud Pie	62
Missouri	65
Burnt Ends	65

Montana	68
Huckleberry Pie	68
Nebraska	71
Runza	71
Nevada	74
Las Vegas Prime Rib Dinner	74
New Hampshire	77
Grape Nuts Ice Cream	77
New Jersey	79
Taylor Ham Sandwich A.K.A. Pork Roll Sandwich	79
New Mexico	81
Green Chili	81
New York	83
Buffalo Chicken Wings	83
North Carolina	86
N.C. Pulled Pork Sandwich	86
North Dakota	90
Kuchen	90
Ohio	93
Cincinnati Chili	93
Oklahoma	96
Chicken Fried Steak	96
Oregon	99
Hazelnut Squash Soup	99
Pennsylvania	101
Philly Cheese Steak	101
Rhode Island	103

- Rhode Island Calamari 103
- South Carolina 106
- Shrimp N' Grits 106
- South Dakota 109
- Chislic 109
- Tennessee 111
- Memphis Sticky Pork Ribs With Corn Hash 111
- Texas 114
- Texas Chili 114
- Utah 117
- Funeral Potatoes 117
- Vermont 119
- Vermont Cheddar Cheese Apple Pie 119
- Virginia 123
- Virginia Ham Biscuits 123
- Washington 126
- Cedar-Planked Salmon 126
- West Virginia 129
- Pepperoni Rolls 129
- Wisconsin 132
- Wisconsin Bratwursts 132
- Wyoming 135
- Wyoming Bison Burgers 135
- Washington D.C. 138
- Chili Half Smokes 138
- Bonus Recipes 141
- Arroz Con Gandules (Puerto Rican Rice With Pigeon Peas) 141

Classic Memphis Bbq Sauce	143
Texas Slow Smoked Brisket	145
Brisket Dry Rub	147
Conclusion	149
Part 2	150
American Carrot Cake Recipe	151
Apple Pie Recipe	153
Apple Pie With Raisin Relish Recipe	155
Banana Split Recipe	157
Blueberry Pancake Recipe	159
Ceviche Recipe	161
Chicken And Fish 65 Burgers Recipe	163
Chilli Burgers With Pepper Relish Recipe	165
Classic American Pancakes Recipe	167
Doughnuts Recipe	169
Ham Rolls Recipe	171
Juicy Lamb Burger Recipe	173
Kfc Style Fried Chicken Recipe	175
Lamb And Pork Burger With Chunky Salad Recipe	177
Lamb Burger With Radish Slaw Recipe	180
Lentil-Mushroom Burgers Recipe	182
Meat Loaf Recipe	185
Potato Corn Burgers Recipe	187

Part 1

Introduction

A great tasting dish, be it a slice of pie or a meal, is something you tell your friends and family about. It is something you want to share so that others can experience the delicious flavors. This is what American regional cooking – and ultimately, this collection of recipes – is truly about.

These dishes are the cuisine each American state is famous for. They reflect the unique regional food cultures that exist across America. These are iconic recipes for traditional dishes which have been passed down for generations so that we can taste their incredible flavors today. It is what is served at the family table, in local restaurants, and at holiday get-togethers. Perhaps most important, these dishes are what locals are proud to serve visitors to their region, giving them an experience to remember when they return home.

Let this collection of recipes serve as a guide for your culinary journey to each state. It will show you the way each state traditionally prepares, cooks and serves its iconic dish, and will enable you to understand how a pie in Georgia differs from a pie in Vermont! With the rich history and culture reflected in each state's official dish, you will discover new variations, methods and flavors in this tasty, filling and delicious journey across America.

Alabama

Fried Green Tomatoes

A Southern delicacy so tasty that you'll want to make it over and over again! This is a traditional recipe for fried green tomatoes coated in cornmeal, which can be served as a starter or as a side.

Serves: 4–6 - Prep Time: 15 minutes - Cook Time: 15 minutes

Ingredients
1 cup stone-ground cornmeal
1 cup all-purpose flour
1 tablespoon garlic powder
1 pinch cayenne pepper
1½ cups buttermilk
Kosher salt and freshly ground black pepper
4 large unripe tomatoes, cut into ½-inch thick slices
½ cup vegetable oil

For serving
Dipping sauce of your choice
Lemon wedges

Directions
1. Pour the buttermilk into a bowl and season with salt and pepper. Mix well.
2. In a shallow bowl, mix the cornmeal, flour, garlic powder and cayenne pepper.
3. Dredge the tomato slices in buttermilk and then through the dry mixture.
4. Heat oil in a deep, heavy-bottomed skillet over medium heat. Fry the tomatoes in batches until golden brown. Avoid overcrowding the skillet so they can cook evenly.
5. Drain the fried tomatoes on paper towels.
6. Once the fried tomatoes have cooled, serve with lemon wedges and your chosen dipping sauce.

Nutrition Information (1 slice)
Calories 74, Total Fat 4g, Saturated Fat 1g, Carbs 5g, Fiber 1g, Sugars 1g, Sodium 33mg, Protein 1g

Alaska

King Salmon Bake

This state's prized fish is the King Salmon, and this is the most requested Alaskan recipe, a delicious baked King Salmon with a delicately balanced honey and mustard sauce. Try this recipe for perfectly baked salmon every time.

Serves: 4 - Prep Time: 5 minutes - Cook Time: 12–15 minutes

Ingredients
4 Alaska King Salmon fillets (with the skin)
Salt and freshly ground black pepper
2 tablespoons Dijon-style mustard
2 tablespoons melted butter
1 tablespoon honey
¼ cup fresh breadcrumbs
¼ cup finely chopped pecans

3 tablespoons fresh chopped parsley (divided; 1 tablespoon for garnish)

Directions
1. Preheat the oven to 400°F and line a baking sheet with parchment paper.
2. Season the Alaska King Salmon fillets with salt and pepper.
3. In a shallow dish, combine the breadcrumbs, pecans and 2 tablespoons of the parsley.
4. In another bowl, mix Dijon mustard, butter, and honey to make the honey mustard mixture.
5. Place the salmon on the parchment paper, skin-side down.
6. Lightly brush the honey mustard mixture over the flesh side of the salmon, ensuring it is well coated with the sticky honey sauce.
7. Take the combined breadcrumb mixture and pat it on top of the sticky sauce, ensuring the salmon fillets are evenly coated.
8. Bake in the oven for 12–15 minutes until cooked through, depending on the thickness of the fillets.
9. Remove from the oven, sprinkle with parsley, if desired, and serve.

Nutrition Information
Calories 415, Total Fat 18g, Saturated Fat 5g, Carbs 27g, Fiber 3g, Sugars 4.4g, Sodium 350mg, Protein 40g,

Arizona

Chimichingas

Considered to be the 'soul food' of Arizona, chimichangas are taken seriously by locals. This is a deep-fried chimichanga with a chicken-and-melted-cheese filling. One you try this traditional chimichanga recipe, you'll understand its legendary status in Arizona.

Serves: 8 - Prep Time: 15 minutes - Cook Time: 20 minutes

Ingredients
8 flour tortillas
1 ½ pounds cooked chicken breast, shredded
1 medium onion, chopped
½ teaspoon garlic powder
1 tablespoon chili powder
¼ teaspoon ground oregano

½ teaspoon ground cumin
Salt and pepper to taste
2 tablespoons vegetable oil
Vegetable oil (for deep frying)
1 (4½-ounce) can green chilies, chopped
2 cups shredded cheddar cheese

Garnish
Salsa (optional)
Sour cream (optional)
Guacamole (optional)

Directions
1. Wrap the stack of tortillas and heat according to instructions.
2. Place a large skillet over medium heat and heat the oil. Add the onion and cook until translucent.
3. Add the drained green chilies and cook for 1–2 minutes, stirring. Add in the shredded chicken and then mix in the cumin, chili powder and garlic powder.
4. Season the chicken mixture with salt and pepper and continue cook on a low heat for 3–4 minutes, stirring continuously. Set the pan aside, allowing the mixture to cool.
5. Preheat the deep fryer to 375°F.
6. Scoop some shredded cheese and then spoon the chicken mixture into the center of each tortilla. Don't overfill, as it will expand.

7. Carefully fold the ends of each tortilla, and then the sides, over the center to ensure the mixture doesn't spill. As they are going into the deep fryer, use a toothpick to secure each chimichanga. Fry until golden brown, about 1½–2 minutes per side.
8. Place the chimichangas on a plate lined with paper towels to drain excess oil.
9. Sprinkle with additional cheese on top, let melt, and serve with sides of sour cream, salsa, and guacamole dip, if desired.

Nutrition Information
Calories 553, Total Fat 38g, Saturated Fat 12g, Carbs 29g,
Fiber 2g, Sugars 2g, Sodium 690mg, Protein 23g

Arkansas

Deep-Fried Catfish

Arkansas's state dish, this Southern-style catfish recipe is a true classic. Perfectly seasoned, breaded and pan-fried catfish is full of flavor and easy to make.
Serves: 4 - Prep Time: 15 minutes - Cook Time: 18 minutes

Ingredients
Batter
1 cup all-purpose flour
1 cup cornmeal
1 tablespoon baking powder
1 teaspoon salt
⅛ teaspoon cayenne pepper (more if you like it spicier)
1 (12-ounce) bottle amber beer

Other ingredients
4 catfish fillets, about 6 ounces each
½ teaspoon salt

½ teaspoon cracked black pepper
1 teaspoon garlic powder
Juice of one lemon
Lemon wedges, for serving
Peanut or vegetable oil for frying

Directions
1. Preheat the deep fryer to 350°F.
2. To make the batter, combine the cornmeal, flour and baking powder and whisk well. Add the salt and cayenne pepper. Whisk until everything is well combined and slowly add in the beer, stirring well until you get a smooth mixture (about 2–3 minutes).
3. Slice the catfish fillets in strips and season with salt and pepper.
4. Sprinkle the garlic powder over the strips.
5. Dredge each strip through the batter, ensuring both sides are evenly coated.
6. Fry in batches until golden brown, being careful not to overcrowd the fryer.
7. Drain the fillets on paper towels and season with salt and pepper and lemon juice.
8. Place on a serving platter and serve with lemon or lime wedges.

Nutrition Information
Calories 199, Total Fat 12g, Saturated Fat 6g, Carbs 14g, Fiber 1g, Sugars 0g, Sodium 244mg, Protein 16g

California

Fish Tacos

Californians love their tacos, and their must-have favorite is the distinctive fish taco, originating from Baja, California. Learn how to make perfectly tasty and delicious fish tacos with this recipe.

Serves: 4 - Prep Time: 10 minutes - Cook Time: 5 minutes

Ingredients
1 tablespoon lime juice
2 teaspoons olive oil
¾ teaspoon chili powder
¾ teaspoon coriander powder
¼ teaspoon salt
3 (4-ounce) fillets of any white fish, such as catfish, mahi mahi, grouper, tilapia, haddock or cod
2 cups thinly shredded green cabbage

2 scallions, thinly sliced
½ cup red onion, finely diced
½ cup diced tomatoes
⅓ cup fresh cilantro, coarsely chopped
8 corn tortillas, warmed
1 ripe avocado, peeled and cut in 8 wedges (optional)
½ lime, juiced (for optional avocado)
Salt and pepper, to taste (optional)

Directions
1. Spray a 9×11-inch baking dish with non-stick spray.
2. Place the fish in the baking tray, skin side down.
3. In a small bowl, squeeze the lime juice and then mix in the chili powder, coriander, and salt and pepper.
4. Brush the mixture over the fish and cover the dish with plastic wrap. Microwave for 3 minutes (high) until the fish is opaque.
5. Take the fish, break it into flakes, and mix in a bowl with olive oil, scallions, red onion, diced tomatoes, and cilantro.
6. To prepare the fish tacos, take a warm tortilla and spoon in equal amounts of the fish mixture and thinly sliced cabbage. Fold the tortilla closed.
7. Place the tortillas on a serving platter and serve with sliced avocado.

Nutrition Information
Calories 257.9, Total Fat 5.2g, Saturated Fat 0.9g, Carbs 27.4g,
Fiber 4.9g, Sugars 2.8g, Sodium 233.1mg, Protein 26.1g

Colorado

Colorado River Trout

Master Colorado's favorite campsite recipe: pan-fried trout, coated in cornmeal and sprinkled with bacon. It's a simple recipe that delivers big flavor.

Serves: 2 - Prep Time: 5 minutes - Cook Time: 10–15 minutes

Ingredients
1 pound bacon, thick-cut strips
2 white onions, thinly sliced
2 freshly caught pan-sized trout or rainbow trout fillets
½ cup cornmeal
½ cup flour
Salt and pepper to season
1 lemon, cut into wedges, for garnish

Directions
1. Dice the bacon.
2. In a large cast iron skillet over medium heat, fry the diced bacon. Remove from the pan, allowing the bacon to drain on a plate lined with paper towels.

3. In the same pan, sauté the onions in the remaining bacon grease until translucent, about 2 minutes. Remove the onions from the skillet and set aside with the bacon. Cover with foil to keep warm.
4. In a shallow dish mix the cornmeal, flour, salt and pepper and whisk until well combined.
5. Prepare the fish by dredging through the flour mixture.
6. Place the trout in the hot pan where the bacon and onion were fried and fry until cooked through (this will depend on the thickness of the fish).
7. Remove the fish from the pan carefully. Sprinkle bacon and sautéed onions on top and serve with lemon wedges.

Nutrition Information (321g per serving)
Calories 715, Total Fat 54g, Saturated Fat 16g, Carbs 30g,
Fiber 2g, Sugars 2g, Sodium 1570mg, Protein 50g

Connecticut

New Haven Steamed White Clam Pizza

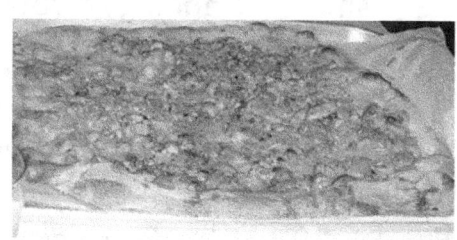

New Haven serves a pizza that has well earned its legendary status in this state. Try this recipe for a delicious thin crust pizza topped with clams, oregano and garlic.

Serves: 2–4 - Prep Time: 2 hours 15 minutes - Cook Time: 10–12 minutes

Ingredients
Crust
¾ cup warm water
1½ teaspoons active dry yeast
1 teaspoon sugar
2¼ cups all-purpose flour, plus more for kneading
1 teaspoon salt
2 tablespoons olive oil, plus some more for greasing

Pizza topping

¾ cup grated Pecorino Romano cheese
1 tablespoon dried oregano
½ cup extra virgin olive oil
4 garlic cloves, minced
¾ cup chopped clams

Directions
1. To make basic dough for the pizza, take a large bowl and mix in the water, yeast and sugar. Whisk together, then set aside for 10 minutes for the yeast to activate.
2. In another bowl, combine the salt and flour and whisk together. Using your fist, make a hole in the center, and pour in the activated yeast mix. Add the olive oil. Mix the ingredients until well combined.
3. On a floured surface, knead the dough for 4–5 minutes until smooth.
4. Take a separate bowl and grease generously with olive oil. Add the dough and cover with plastic wrap. Set aside in a warm area. Let rest until the dough has doubled in size.
5. Preheat the oven to 400°F.
6. Drain the clams of most of the excess liquid and place them in a bowl. Drizzle with olive oil, garlic and oregano and mix gently.
7. When the dough has doubled, shape it in either round or rectangle thin crust. Transfer it to a baking sheet of corresponding shape. Sprinkle the pizza base with the cheese and the clam mixture so that the pizza is topped evenly.

8. Place in the oven and bake until golden brown, about 10–15 minutes.

Nutrition Information (1 slice)
Calories 300, Total Fat 12g, Saturated Fat 2g, Carbs 8g, Fiber 0.3g, Sugars 0.9g, Sodium 300mg, Protein 45g

Delaware

Scrapple

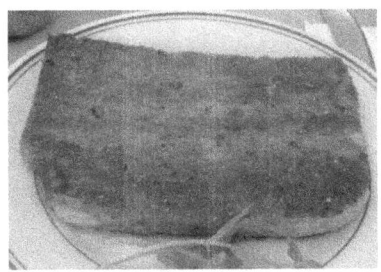

This dish is so iconic that Delaware even has an Apple Scrapple Festival dedicated to it every October! It's like tasty slices of seasoned pork. To make scrapple, follow this traditional recipe and serve instead of bacon or sausage for breakfast.

Serves: 4–6 - Prep Time: 15 minutes - Cook Time: 10 minutes

Ingredients
1 ½ pounds ground beef
2 cups yellow cornmeal
¼ teaspoon basil
2 teaspoons sage
1 tablespoon salt
½ teaspoon garlic powder
½ teaspoon marjoram

1 tablespoon black pepper
1½ teaspoons nutmeg
A pinch of clove powder
½ cup water
½ teaspoon onion powder

Directions
1. Place a pot over medium heat and add the hamburger meat and some water. Cook the meat until tender and almost grey.
2. Drain the juice from the hamburger meat and keep half the juice to use as stock.
3. In another pot, bring the stock to a boil and add the cornmeal, stirring quickly.
4. When the stock has thickened, add the hamburger meat and fully incorporate into the mixture.
5. Add the remaining seasonings and continue to stir for approximately 30 minutes.
6. Remove from heat and pour the hamburger meat carefully into loaf pans. Place in refrigerator for 6–8 hours or overnight so that it solidifies.
7. Before serving, slice the scrapple in ½-inch-thick slices and fry it in a frying pan. You can serve it with your favorite dipping sauce or as a side to your breakfast eggs.

Nutrition Information (1 slice)
Calories 57, Total Fat 3.6g, Saturated Fat 1.25g, Carbs 3.74g,
Fiber 0g, Sugars 0g, Sodium 132mg, Protein 2.14g

Florida

Key Lime Pie

A light and refreshing pie that strikes the perfect balance of sweet and tart, this is a classic and all-time favorite directly from Florida Keys.

Serves: 8 - Prep Time: 30 minutes - Cook Time: 10–12 minutes

Ingredients
1 prepared graham cracker crust (9 inches) or basic graham crust recipe
3 egg yolks
1 teaspoon grated lime zest
1 (14-ounce) can sweetened condensed milk
¾ cup freshly squeezed key lime juice
1 cup whipping cream
1 teaspoon vanilla extract
3 tablespoons confectioners' sugar

Directions
1. To prepare the filling, add the egg yolks to a large electric mixing bowl and beat until light and fluffy, about 4 minutes on medium speed. Add the lime zest and continue beating for 1 minute on high speed.
2. Reduce speed to medium and add the condensed milk. Beat for 4–5 more minutes until creamy and smooth.
3. Add the key lime juice, and mix just to blend all the ingredients together.
4. Preheat the oven to 350°F. Take the filling and pour it into the pie crust carefully. Place in the oven and bake for 10–12 minutes or until the lime custard sets. Remove from the oven and let cool down before refrigerating for 2–3 hours before serving. Alternatively, you could place it in the freezer for 20 minutes.
5. Meanwhile, to make the topping, take a small mixing bowl and whip the cream so that it forms peaks. Add the sugar and vanilla and whisk until it stiffens. Refrigerate.
6. Before serving, you can either pipe the topping around the pie or spread it evenly over the filling.

Nutrition Information (1 slice)
Calories 364, Total Fat 16g, Saturated Fat 4g, Carbs 49g, Fiber 1g, Sugars 26g, Sodium 309mg, Protein 5g

Georgia

Lattice Top Georgia Peach Pie

The Peach State's favorite pie could be no other than a lattice top Georgia peach pie. A flaky crust and fresh peaches make for a crisp pie and a gooey filling, a pie so good it will feature at most Georgia picnics and barbecues this summer.

Serves: 10 - Prep Time: 45 minutes - Cook Time: 75 minutes

Ingredients
Prepared pastry for a double-crust 10-inch pie
3 pounds Georgia peaches
1 cup sugar (divided, plus some more for dusting)
1 tablespoon cornstarch

4 tablespoons all-purpose flour
1 teaspoon fresh lime juice
½ teaspoon cinnamon
1 pinch salt
1½ tablespoons cold butter
1½ tablespoons heavy cream
Vanilla ice cream or whipping cream for serving (optional)

Directions
1. Remove the stones from the peaches, peel and slice evenly. Place in a large mixing bowl. Add half the sugar and stir a few times. Set aside for 20 minutes. Drain the peaches in a strainer placed over a small saucepan. Bring the juice from the peaches to a boil over medium-high heat until it reduces and thickens, about 3–4 minutes. Set aside and let cool down.
2. Place the peaches back in the mixing bowl. Add the cornstarch, flour, cinnamon, lime juice, and a pinch of salt. Also add the reserved peach juices. Stir until all ingredients are well combined.
3. Prepare the pie base by lightly dusting a surface with flour. Taking half the pie dough, roll it out in a round circle of about 11 inches in diameter. Place in a 10-inch pie pan and allow for some of the dough to hang over the edges. Take the remaining dough disk and refrigerate.

4. Pour the filling into the pie crust and, using a teaspoon, spoon small knobs of butter over the filling (just to dot).
5. Preheat the oven to 350°F and line a baking sheet with aluminum foil.
6. Meanwhile, take the remaining dough and roll out on a lightly dusted surface in a round circle of about 11 inches in diameter. Take a knife and cut strips of about 1 inch wide. Take the strips and weave the lattice crust over the top of the pie, allowing for the ends to overhang.
7. Flute the edges to seal around the pie and cut away any excess.
8. Bake in the oven for 30 minutes. Remove the pie from the oven, brush the crust with cream and lightly sprinkle sugar.
9. Return to the oven for another 30–45 minutes, or until the pie is cooked through, bubbly and golden.
10. Allow to cool before slicing. The pie filling will be piping hot. Serve with whipped cream or vanilla ice cream, if desired.

Nutrition Information (1 slice)
Calories 325, Total Fat 14g, Saturated Fat 4g, Carbs 47g, Fiber 2g, Sugars 28g, Sodium 223mg, Protein 3g

Hawaii

Ahi Poke

Food is a way of life in Hawaii. Ahi poke is one of the most beloved dish found in Hawaiian restaurant throughout the state. Ahi poke is composed of marinated cubes of ahi tuna in a perfect blend of spices.
Serves: 6-8 - Prep Time: 15 minutes plus chill time - Cook Time: none

Ingredients
1 pound ahi tuna, cut into evenly sized small chunks
½ cup soy sauce
2 teaspoons sesame oil
1 tablespoon garlic chili paste
½ cup sweet onion, sliced thin
2 teaspoons toasted sesame seeds
2 cloves garlic, crushed and minced
1 tablespoon fresh ginger, grated
2 teaspoons fresh lemongrass, finely chopped
Lettuce leaves for serving

Scallions, sliced, for garnish
Macadamia nuts, chopped, for garnish

Directions
1. In a bowl, combine the soy sauce, sesame oil, and garlic chili paste. Whisk well until blended.
2. Stir in the onion, sesame seeds, garlic, ginger, and lemongrass.
3. Add the tuna and toss to coat evenly.
4. Cover the bowl and place in the refrigerator for 30-60 minutes.
5. Serve in or with lettuce leaves and garnish with a sprinkling of scallions and macadamia nuts before serving, if desired.

Nutrition Information (3 ounces)
Calories 250, Total Fat 10g, Saturated Fat 0g, Carbs 3g, Fiber 0g, Sugars 0g, Sodium 1043mg, Protein 14g

Idaho

Finger Steak

This state's dish is well loved by locals and the many visitors who try it on their travels. It consists of strips of steak, seasoned, battered and deep fried. Try this original recipe for finger steaks that are perfect every time.

Serves: 4 - Prep Time: 3 hours 30 minutes - Cook Time: 10 minutes

Ingredients
1½ pounds sirloin steak, boneless and ¼ inch thick
Fry sauce for serving

Wet dredging batter
1 egg
2 cups buttermilk

2 tablespoons steak seasoning
½ cup all-purpose flour

Dry dredging mix
2½ cups all-purpose flour
2 teaspoons garlic powder
Salt and pepper
3 cups canola oil for deep frying

Directions
1. Cut the beef in 2-inch strips.
2. Add all the ingredients for the wet dredging batter to a large mixing bowl. Whisk well until the batter becomes smooth.
3. Add the beef strips to the batter mixture and chill in the refrigerator for 2 hours.
4. Add all the dry dredging mix ingredients to a shallow bowl and stir until well combined.
5. Remove the steak strips from the batter, shake off the excess batter, and dredge the strips into the flour mixture, ensuring they are evenly coated.
6. For better results, place the steak strips in an even layer on a baking sheet and freeze for 1 hour. This will help keep the batter stuck to the steak strips as it fries.
7. Pour oil in a deep thick-bottomed pan and heat over medium heat until it reaches 375°F. (You can also use a deep fryer.)
8. Remove the steak strips from the freezer and fry in batches until golden brown, about 5 minutes. If you

fry the strips without freezing them, reduce the frying time to 2–3 minutes. Be careful to avoid overcrowding the pan or deep fryer.
9. Place the finger steaks on a plate lined with paper towels to drain the excess oil.
10. Transfer to a serving platter and serve with fry sauce for dipping.

Nutrition Information
Calories 825, Total Fat 35g, Saturated Fat 10g, Carbs 80g,
Fiber 3g, Sugars 7g, Sodium 1588mg, Protein 47g

Illinois

Chicago-Style Deep-Dish Pizza

A traditional Chicago-style pizza is more than a pizza: Its base is a pie with a deep, flaky and crunchy crust. Follow this recipe for an authentic deep-dish pie crust, filled with a rich tomato sauce with a hint of heat.

Yields: 2 pizzas (9-inch) - Prep Time: 2 hours 20 minutes - Cook Time: 30 minutes

Ingredients
Crust
2¼ teaspoons instant or rapid-rise yeast
2 teaspoons sugar
½ cup yellow cornmeal
3¼ cups all-purpose flour, plus some more for kneading
1½ teaspoons salt
1¼ cups water, room temperature
3 tablespoons melted butter, unsalted
1 teaspoon olive oil, plus more for greasing pans

4 tablespoons semolina

Tomato sauce
2 tablespoons unsalted butter
½ teaspoon crushed red pepper flakes
1 small onion, finely diced
¾ teaspoon salt
1 teaspoon dried oregano
¼ teaspoon granulated sugar
3 garlic cloves, minced
1 (28-ounce) can crushed tomatoes

Toppings for pizzas
4 cups shredded mozzarella cheese
½ cup grated parmesan cheese
Toppings: cooked and crumbled sausages, sliced pepperoni, thinly sliced green peppers, onions or mushrooms

Directions
Making the pizza crust
1. In a large bowl, mix the yeast, sugar, cornmeal, flour and salt until combined. Slowly add in the water and melted butter and mix well until all the ingredients have been combined.
2. Lightly flour a surface with semolina and knead the dough for about 5 minutes.
3. Grease a separate bowl with 1 teaspoon of olive oil. Take the dough and place it in the greased bowl,

turning it over several times to ensure that all sides are oiled.
4. Cover the bowl with plastic wrap and set aside in a warm area to rest and double in size.

Making the tomato sauce

5. In the meantime, prepare the tomato based sauce. Melt 2 tablespoons unsalted butter in a saucepan over medium heat. As it is melting, add the pepper flakes, onion, salt and oregano. Stir until the onion has slightly browned. Turn the heat to low and add in the sugar, garlic and tomatoes. Allow to simmer on low heat for 30 minutes until it has reduced and thickened.

Making the pizzas

6. Preheat the oven to 425°F and grease two 9-inch round cake pans with olive oil.
7. Slightly flour a surface with semolina or flour and roll the dough out thickly into a round shape of about 13 inches diameter (it must be larger than the cake pans so that the dough can cover the sides as well). Gently push the rolled dough into the bottom of the cake pans and up the sides.
8. To top the pizzas, first add about 2 cups of cheese over the surface of each crust, then pour on 1 cup of the sauce (or less, depending on preference) and finally sprinkle each with the parmesan cheese.

9. Toppings: You can add any toppings you prefer, such as sliced peppers, pepperoni, sausage, sliced mushrooms, or more cheese.
10. Place the pizzas in the oven and bake for 28–30 minutes or until the crusts are golden brown.
11. Remove from the oven and allow to cool (the topping will be piping hot) before serving.

Nutrition Information (1 slice)
Calories 310, Total Fat 16g, Saturated Fat 5g, Carbs 28g, Fiber 2g, Sugars 2g, Sodium 340mg, Protein 14g

Indiana

Breaded Pork Tenderloin Sandwich

Indiana's breaded pork tenderloin sandwich is so good that it is served almost everywhere statewide. This iconic Midwestern sandwich features pork steak that is seasoned, breaded and pan-fried. It's quick, easy and big on flavor.

Serves: 2–4 - Prep Time: 30 minutes - Cook Time: 20 minutes

Ingredients
4 pork tenderloins, about 4 ounces each
1 egg, beaten
4 tablespoons milk
1½ cups bread crumbs
¼ teaspoon dried marjoram
¼ teaspoon dried oregano
¼ teaspoon garlic powder
¼ teaspoon onion powder

½ teaspoon salt
¼ teaspoon black pepper
½ cup peanut oil for frying
4 Kaiser rolls, split
4 teaspoons of mayonnaise, ketchup or yellow mustard for dressing (optional)
4 leaves lettuce
4 slices tomato
4 slices onion
4 slices pickle

Directions
1. Prepare the pork tenderloins by pounding them between two plastic sheets until about ¼ inch thick.
2. In a shallow dish, beat the egg and milk until well combined.
3. To a separate bowl, add the breadcrumbs, marjoram, oregano, garlic powder, onion powder, salt and pepper. Stir to combine.
4. Dip the cutlets into the wet mixture and then dredge them through the breadcrumb mixture until each cutlet is evenly coated on both sides.
5. Place a large, deep heavy-bottomed skillet over medium-high heat and heat the oil therein.
6. Fry each cutlet until brown and cooked through, about 6–7 minutes on each side.
7. Drain the cutlets on a plate lined with paper towels.
8. Meanwhile, preheat the grill or oven broiler and toast the Kaiser rolls on each side.

9. To prepare the sandwiches, place a cutlet on the bottom of each bun. Add your preferred dressing and the onion, lettuce, tomato and pickle. Top with the other half of the bun.
10. Place the breaded pork tenderloin sandwiches on a platter and serve.

Nutrition Information (1 serving)
Calories 703, Total 29g, Saturated Fat 11g, Carbs 87g, Fiber 3g, Sugars 15g, Sodium 1.6mg, Protein 29g

Iowa

Loose Meat Sandwich

Another iconic Midwestern sandwich, the loose meat sandwich is Iowa's claim to fame. A seasoned ground beef sandwich served on buns, it's a quick and easy recipe that makes for a satisfying meal.
Serves: 6 - Prep Time: 15 minutes - Cook Time: 55 minutes

Ingredients
2 tablespoons oil
2 small onions, diced thinly (reserve some for garnish)
2 pounds extra-lean ground beef
2 tablespoons yellow mustard
2 tablespoons white vinegar
2 tablespoons Worcestershire sauce
4 teaspoons sugar
½ teaspoon garlic powder
Salt and pepper to taste
2 (14.5-ounce) cans low-sodium beef broth

6 hamburger buns
Sliced pickles (optional)
Fries or potato chips for serving

Directions
1. Place a large skillet over medium-high heat and heat the oil therein. Add the onions and sauté until fragrant and translucent, about 2 minutes. Add the ground beef. Using a wooden spoon, break up any lumps and cook until cooked through, about 3–5 minutes.
2. Add the broth, white vinegar, mustard, Worcestershire sauce, sugar, garlic, salt, and pepper. Mix until incorporated with the beef and onions.
3. Bring the mixture to a boil and reduce heat to low. Let the beef mixture simmer uncovered until all the liquid evaporates, about 30–40 minutes.
4. Toast the hamburger buns under a broiler or on the grill until warm.
5. To serve, spoon the beef mixture directly onto the buns. Add pickles and onions, if desired.
6. Place the loose meat sandwiches on a platter and serve with a side of fries or chips.

Nutrition Information (1 burger and roll)
Calories 332, Total Fat 13g, Saturated Fat 5g, Carbs 23g, Fiber 1g, Sugars 4g, Sodium 923mg, Protein 28g

Kansas

Kansas-City-Style Ribs

This traditional Kansas-style rib recipe features a dry rub, big flavors and a great spicy sauce that sets it apart from other barbecue ribs and gives it an authentic Kansas City flavor.

Serves: 6+ - Prep Time: 15 minutes, plus 1–12 hours marinating time - Cook Time: 5 hours 20 minutes

Ingredients
3 slabs baby back pork ribs
Favorite sides for serving

Rub ingredients
2 cups brown sugar
½ cup dry mustard
1 tablespoon cayenne pepper
1 tablespoon smoked paprika
1 tablespoon garlic powder

1 tablespoon onion powder
1 tablespoon celery salt
1 tablespoon salt
2 teaspoons freshly ground black pepper

Barbecue sauce
2 tablespoons vegetable oil
1 onion, finely diced
3 cups water
1 cup tomato paste
½ cup brown sugar
⅔ cup apple cider vinegar
¼ cup molasses
¼ teaspoon cayenne pepper
¼ teaspoon smoked paprika
1 teaspoon salt
1 teaspoon freshly ground black pepper

Directions
1. Prepare the ribs by patting them down with paper towels to remove any excess moisture. Remove the white membrane with a paring knife.
2. Mix all the rub ingredients in a bowl and apply generously to all sides of the ribs so that they are heavily coated. Place the ribs in the refrigerator for at least 1 and up to 12 hours.
3. Prepare the barbeque sauce by heating the oil over low heat in a saucepan. Add the diced onion and sauté for 1–2 minutes. When the onion is translucent, add the water, tomato paste, vinegar,

molasses, cayenne pepper, paprika, salt, and pepper. Bring to a boil, reduce heat to low, and allow to simmer for 30 minutes.
4. Cook the ribs in a smoker for 3–4 hours, turning and basting with the sauce every 40 minutes, until the ribs are cooked through and tender.
5. Place ribs on a serving platter and serve with your favorite sides.

Note: To cook the ribs in an oven, preheat the oven to 350°F. Baste the ribs with the sauce and cover with aluminum foil. Repeat the basting process every 30 minutes for 2½ hours. Remove the foil and turn the broiler on for the last 30 minutes.

Nutrition Information (4 ounces)
Calories 260, Total Fat 17g, Saturated Fat 6g, Carbs 6g, Fiber 0g, Sugars 1g, Sodium 600mg, Protein 19g

Kentucky

Kentucky Fried Chicken

This state's recipe is so iconic worldwide that even the secret recipe for it is now out! This traditional and delicious Southern comfort food will satisfy everyone around the table.

Serves: 4 - Prep Time: 30 minutes - Cook Time: 30 minutes

Ingredients
1 whole chicken, cut into pieces, about 3-4 pounds

Wet dredging ingredients
4 eggs
⅓ cup water

Dry dredging ingredients

2 cups all-purpose flour
1 tablespoon baking powder
¼ teaspoon salt

Seasoning
½ tablespoon thyme
½ tablespoon basil
⅓ tablespoon oregano
1 tablespoon celery salt
1 tablespoon black pepper
1 tablespoon dried mustard
⅔ tablespoon salt
4 tablespoons paprika
2 tablespoons garlic powder
1 tablespoon ground ginger
3 tablespoons white pepper

Directions
1. Rinse the chicken pieces and pat them down with paper towels to remove excess water.
2. In a shallow dish, mix the eggs and the water.
3. In another shallow dish, mix the 2 cups of flour, baking powder and ¼ teaspoon salt.
4. To prepare the seasoning, take a medium sized bowl and add the salt, thyme, basil, oregano, celery, salt, black pepper, dried mustard, paprika, garlic powder, ground ginger and white pepper. Whisk until well combined.
5. Sprinkle the chicken with the seasoning so that it is lightly dusted. Add the remaining seasoning mix to

the flour mixture and whisk so that they are well incorporated.
6. Dip the lightly dusted chicken pieces into the wet mixture and then dredge through the flour mixture. Make sure that the chicken pieces are well coated on all sides.
7. Place the pieces on a wire rack.
8. Preheat the deep fryer to 350°F, or add 4 cups of vegetable oil to a deep heavy-bottomed saucepan and heat over medium heat to 350°F. When the oil has reached 350°F, fry the chicken pieces until golden brown and thoroughly cooked through. Avoid overcrowding so that they can cook evenly.
9. The internal temperature for the chicken to be ready is 165°F. This can easily be checked on an instant-read meat thermometer.
10. Place the cooked chicken pieces on a plate lined with paper towels to drain excess oil and keep them crispy. Serve and enjoy.

Nutrition Information (100 g)
Calories 246, Total Fat 12g, Saturated Fat 3g, Carbs 6g, Fiber 1g, Sugars 0g, Sodium 610mg, Protein 20g

Louisiana Jambalaya

Nothing says Louisiana better than a hot steaming and spicy jambalaya. A rich rice dish mixing seafoods, meats, and vegetables with a perfect blend of creole spices.

Serves: 10-12 - Prep Time: 10 minutes - Cook Time: 45 minutes

Ingredients
2 pounds shrimp, cleaned and deveined
½ pound redfish, cubed
½ pound smoked bacon, diced
1 pound pork sausage
1 pound andouille sausage
½ pound dark chicken meat, cubed
¼ cup butter
1 onion, diced
1 bell pepper, diced

1 cup celery, diced
4 cloves garlic, crushed and minced
2 cups long grain white rice, rinsed
1 tablespoon smoked paprika
1 tablespoon celery salt
2 teaspoon thyme
1 tablespoon Creole seasoning
1 teaspoon salt
1 teaspoon black pepper
2 bay leaves
2 cups seafood stock or fish stock
1 ½ cups stewed tomatoes with liquid

Directions
1. Arrange the bacon in a deep skillet or Dutch oven over medium heat. Cook until lightly browned. Add the pork sausage and andouille sausage and cook for approximately 10 minutes.
2. Remove the contents of the skillet with a slotted spoon and set them aside on paper towels to drain.
3. Add the chicken to the skillet and cook, turning occasionally, until browned on all sides. Remove from the skillet and set aside.
4. Melt the butter in the skillet. Add the onion, celery, green pepper, and garlic. Cook for 5 minutes.
5. Next, add the rice and season with the paprika, celery salt, thyme, Creole seasoning, salt, and black pepper. Return all of the cooked meat to the skillet along and add the bay leaves.

6. Add the chicken stock and tomatoes to the skillet and increase the heat to medium high.
7. Bring the liquid to a boil, and then reduce the heat, cover, and simmer for 15-20 minutes.
8. Add the shrimp and redfish. Cover, and cook an additional 10 minutes.
9. Remove from the heat and let it sit for 10 minutes before serving.

Nutrition Information (244 g)
Calories 393, Total Fat 21g, Saturated Fat 7g, Carbs 23g, Fiber 1g, Sugars 2g, Sodium 478mg, Protein 26g

Maine

Lobster Rolls

Maine's fresh lobsters feature in many recipes from this state. The most famous of them is, of course, the lobster roll. Jumbo cold lobster meat stuffed into warm rolls and brushed with butter is a simple and classic Maine recipe that will impress your guests.

Serves: 4 - Prep Time: 10 minutes - Cook Time: 15–20 minutes refrigeration

Ingredients
1 pound lobster meat, cooked and separated into large pieces
3 tablespoons mayonnaise
1 tablespoon freshly squeezed lemon juice
1 celery stalk, finely diced
1 tablespoon fresh chives, finely chopped
1 pinch cayenne (optional)
Salt and freshly ground black pepper
6 New-England-style hot dog rolls
Softened butter

Directions
1. To make the lobster roll filling, use a wooden spoon to break the cooked lobster meat into large chunks.
2. To a mixing bowl, add the mayonnaise, lemon juice, diced celery, chives, and cayenne (if desired). Stir until well combined. Season with salt and freshly cracked black pepper to taste.
3. Add the lobster meat and gently stir to coat. Cover the bowl with plastic wrap and allow the flavors to develop by chilling in the refrigerator for 15–20 minutes.
4. Brush butter on both side of each bun. Warm a large cast iron pan and cook the buns until golden brown on both sides, about 1 minute per side.
5. Open the warmed buns and stuff with the lobster mixture. Place the rolls on a serving platter and enjoy.

Nutrition Information (1 roll)
Calories 316, Total Fat 25g, Saturated Fat 10g, Carbs 33g,
Fiber 1g, Sugars 5g, Sodium 1870mg, Protein 74g

Maryland Crab Cakes

Maryland is famed for its fresh seafood and its delicious crab cakes in particular. Seasoned crabmeat, shaped into crab cakes and seared until they reach golden brown perfection, is a delicious summer dish.

Serves: 3 - Prep Time: 1 hour 15 minutes - Cook Time: 10–12 minutes

Ingredients
1½ pounds lump crabmeat
1½ teaspoons Old Bay seasoning
1 large egg
1 teaspoon fresh lemon juice
¼ cup mayonnaise
1½ teaspoons Dijon style mustard
½ teaspoon Worcestershire sauce
½ teaspoon salt
½ teaspoon freshly cracked black pepper

1¼ cups fresh breadcrumbs
1 tablespoon fresh flat-leaf parsley, chopped
2 tablespoons unsalted butter
1 tablespoon olive oil
Lemon, cut in wedges

Directions
1. Place the crabmeat in a large bowl and break up any chunks with a wooden spoon.
2. In a different bowl, mix the Old Bay seasoning, lemon juice, Worcestershire sauce, salt, pepper, and egg. Whisk until well combined.
3. Add the crabmeat and mix until fully incorporated.
4. Carefully add the breadcrumbs and mix gently with a fork (making sure not to over-mix or solidify).
5. Cover the bowl with plastic wrap and place in the refrigerator for 1 hour to allow the flavors to fully develop.
6. To prepare the crab cakes, divide the mixture evenly into 6 balls and gently flatten them into cakes of about 1 inch thick.
7. Place a large cast iron skillet over medium heat and drizzle in the olive oil. Add the butter and let it melt. Add each crab cake. Cook until golden brown on both sides, about 2–3 minutes for each side.
8. Place the crab cakes on a serving platter around the lemon wedges and serve.

Nutrition Information (2 crab cakes)
Calories 299, Total Fat 14g, Saturated Fat 3g, Carbs 9g,

Fiber 9g, Sugars 1g, Sodium 1141mg, Protein 32g

Massachusetts

New England Clam Chowder

This state serves a chowder distinctive of New England; a rich, hearty and warming chowder with potatoes, onions and clams. This is a traditional recipe that is both easy to make and wholesome.

Serves: 8 - Prep Time: 45 minutes - Cook Time: 30 minutes

Ingredients
3 strips thick-cut bacon, diced
2 pounds fresh or frozen clam meat, with juices, chopped
4 tablespoons unsalted butter
1 large yellow onion, diced
1 celery stalk, diced
1 teaspoon fresh thyme leaves, chopped
2 bay leaves
2 medium-size white potatoes, peeled and cut into cubes

½ cup all-purpose flour
4 cups bottled clam juice
3 cups milk
½ cup heavy cream
½ teaspoon white pepper
1 teaspoon kosher salt

Directions
1. Preheat the oven to 400°F and line a baking sheet with parchment paper.
2. Cook the bacon in a large pot over medium heat. Remove the bacon with a slotted spoon and set aside.
3. Add onions to the pot with the bacon grease and cook until translucent, about 2 minutes.
4. Return the bacon to the pot. Add the diced celery, thyme, bay leaves, butter and flour. Stir until this begins to thicken, and then slowly add in the milk and cream to achieve a nice smooth texture. Add the white pepper.
5. To another pot, add water and the salt. Bring to a boil over high heat. Add the diced potatoes and cook until fork tender. Drain the potatoes.
6. Add the potatoes and the clam meat to the thickened sauce and slowly add in the clam juice. Cook on high heat for 5–8 minutes until the clam meat is cooked. Let it sit on the stove until it thickens to the desired consistency.
7. Serve while hot and enjoy.

Nutrition Information (1 cup)
Calories 161, Total Fat 6.4g, Saturated Fat 2.9g, Carbs 16g,
Fiber 1.5g, Sugars 7.3g, Sodium 976mg, Protein 9.3g

Michigan

Michigan Cherry Pie

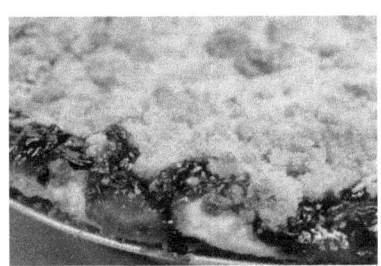

An all-American pie, Michigan's cherry pie has a tart cherry filling and a light, flaky crust that makes it both refreshing and indulgent.

Serves: 8 - Prep Time: 20 minutes - Cook Time: 45 minutes

Ingredients
Crust
Pie dough for 9-inch single crust
¾ cup rolled oats
½ cup all-purpose flour
½ cup packed brown sugar
⅓ cup butter, melted
¼ teaspoon salt

Cherry filling
5 cups fresh cherries, pitted (or frozen tart cherries, thawed and drained)

1¼ cups dried cherries
1 tablespoon lemon juice
½ teaspoon lemon zest
½ teaspoon vanilla extract
1 cup sugar
¼ cup cornstarch

Vanilla ice cream, for serving

Directions
1. Preheat the oven to 375°F.
2. Prepare the pie crust by lightly dusting a surface with flour, then rolling the pastry out in a thick, round circle of 10–11 inches. Place this in a 9-inch pie plate and allow some of the dough to hang over the edge for now.
3. For the filling, mix the sugar and corn starch in a large bowl. Add in the lemon juice, lemon zest, fresh or frozen cherries, and dried cherries. Mix to make sure the cherries are well coated. Pour the mixture into the pie crust.
4. In another bowl, mix the rolled oats, the brown sugar, melted butter, salt and flour. Lightly sprinkle this over the pie filling.
5. Flute the edges to seal around the pie and cut away any excess.
6. Bake in the oven for 30 minutes, until golden brown.
7. Carefully remove from the oven. Allow pie to cool before serving, as the filling will be piping hot.

8. Serve with a scoop of vanilla ice cream.

Nutrition Information (1 slice)
Calories 390, Total Fat 16.5g, Saturated Fat 3.8g, Carbs 59.7g,
Fiber 1.2g, Sugars 21.4, Sodium 369mg, Protein 3g

Minnesota

Minnesota Hot Dish

Minnesotans certainly know how to make a tasty casserole. Known to locals only as "hot dish", in Minnesota this dish traditionally consists of ground beef and cream of mushroom layered with tater tots and melted cheese. Try this quick and easy recipe and it will win you over too.

Serves: 4–6 - Prep Time: 10 minutes - Cook Time: 45 minutes

Ingredients
1 tablespoon olive oil, plus some more for greasing
1 onion, diced
1 pound ground beef
½ teaspoon garlic powder
Salt and freshly ground black pepper, to taste
1 (10¾-ounce) can cream of mushroom soup
1 (10¾-ounce) can cream of chicken soup
½ cup milk

1 (16-ounce) package frozen vegetables such as corn, beans or peas
1 (16-ounce) package frozen tater tots
1½ cups Monterrey Jack or cheddar cheese, shredded

Directions
1. Preheat the oven to 350°F. Grease a 9×13-inch baking dish with some olive oil.
2. Warm 1 tablespoon of olive oil in a large deep skillet over medium heat. Sauté the diced onions for about 2 minutes until translucent and fragrant. Add the beef and garlic powder. Season with salt and pepper. Brown the beef until cooked through. Drain the excess liquids.
3. Add the vegetables and stir.
4. In a small bowl, mix the milk and both soups. Pour over the vegetables-and-beef mixture. Stir to combine. Spread the mixture in the baking dish with a spatula.
5. Layer the tater tots on top and bake in the oven for 30 minutes.
6. Remove from the oven and sprinkle the cheese over the tater tots. Bake until the cheese is melted and casserole edges are bubbly, about 15 minutes.
7. Allow to stand for 5 minutes before serving.

Nutrition Information (1 serving)
Calories 353, Total Fat 15.3g, Saturated Fat 4.9g, Carbs 27.4g,
Fiber 3.2g, Sugars 1.9g, Sodium 1071mg, Protein 23.8g

Mississippi

Mississippi Mud Pie

A classic American dessert, the Mississippi mud pie is a rich chocolate filling cake with a crumbly crust, topped with cream and sprinkles. The recipe for this decadent dessert from Mississippi is one you'll want to try this summer.

Serves: 6 - Prep Time: 15 minutes - Cook Time: 60 minutes

Ingredients
Pie crust
12 chocolate graham crackers
4 tablespoons unsalted butter, melted, plus more if needed
2 tablespoons granulated sugar

Chocolate custard
¾ cup unsalted butter, at room temperature
1¾ cups light brown sugar
4 large eggs
4 tablespoons unsweetened cocoa
⅔ cup semi-sweet chocolate chips
1¼ cups heavy cream
2 teaspoons chocolate extract

Toppings
Whipped cream
Chocolate curls

Cooking spray

Directions
1. Preheat the oven to 350°F and grease a 9-inch spring form pan with cooking spray.
2. To make the pie crust, break the graham crackers into crumbs by placing them into a freezer bag and crushing with a rolling pin. Place the crumb mixture into a bowl and make a well in the center with your hand. Pour in the 4 tablespoons of melted butter, add the sugar, and mix well. If you notice the mixture is still dry, add another tablespoon of melted butter. It should have a moist texture.
3. Gently press the pie crust into the greased spring form pan. Place in the oven and bake for 10–12 minutes, until the crust is lightly toasted. Reduce the temperature of the oven to 325°F.

4. In a mixing bowl, beat the ¾ cup of butter and the brown sugar. Add the eggs, one at a time, and continue beating until smooth and fluffy.
5. In a smaller bowl, melt the chocolate chips in the microwave. Mix into the filling mixture and beat to combine. Slowly add the heavy cream, chocolate extract, and cocoa. Beat for another 3–4 minutes until you have a smooth, lump-free mixture.
6. Add the filling mixture to the crust and bake in the oven for 45 minutes at 325°F.
7. Allow the mud pie to cool completely before topping with whipped cream and chocolate curls. Serve and enjoy.

Nutrition Information (1 serving, 8.5 ounces)
Calories 679, Total Fat 32g, Saturated Fat 17g, Carbs 90g,
Fiber 3g, Sugars 57.28g, Sodium 395mg, Protein 8.58g

Missouri

Burnt Ends

Burnt ends are a Kansas City tradition. These meaty bits are cut off of the point half on a smoked brisket. Once the brisket has been smoked, the ends are removed and cooked longer. This recipe includes a sweet and spicy rub that adds flavor to the crispy "bark" of the burnt ends.

Serves: 6 - Prep Time: 45 minutes - Cook Time: 6 hours

Ingredients:
1 beef brisket, about 5 pounds, trimmed and membrane removed
1 cup brown sugar
½ cup white sugar
½ cup paprika
¼ cup chili powder
3 tablespoons garlic powder
3 tablespoons ground cumin
2 tablespoons black pepper
1 tablespoon cayenne

Directions:
1. Prepare the smoker and bring to a temperature of about 220°F.
2. In a bowl, combine all the ingredients for the rub: brown sugar, white sugar, paprika, chili powder, garlic powder, cumin, pepper, and cayenne. Mix well, making sure that that the brown sugar is completely broken up and no longer clumpy.
3. Trim the fat off the brisket. Place wood chips in the smoker. If you desire a heavier smoked taste, burn off the wood chips to create more smoke.
4. Pat the brisket liberally with the rub and place on the grill. Cook the brisket for about an hour per pound, rotating every 30 minutes. Use a meat thermometer inserted into the middle of the brisket to check temperature before removing from the heat. Let the brisket sit for 15 minutes before removing the burnt ends.
5. To remove the burnt ends, find the layer of fat that separates the burnt end tip from the rest of the brisket. With a sharp knife, carefully slice into the layer of fat and remove the end. Return the end piece to the grill and continue to cook for an additional hour. The tip will have a thick bark on it and appear almost burnt. Remove from the heat and let rest 15 minutes before cutting.
6. Cut the meat into slightly larger than bite size pieces to serve.

Nutrition Information

Calories 680, Total Fat 34g, Saturated Fat 13g, Carbs 61g,
Fiber 1g, Sugars 37g, Sodium 1700mg, Protein 34g

Montana

Huckleberry Pie

Montana is known for its tasty huckleberries, and the state's recipe for huckleberry pie is a truly delicious dessert. A tart wild huckleberry filling and a flaky, crumbly crust make a perfectly balance of sweet and tangy.
Serves: 6 - Prep Time: 20 minutes - Cook Time: 90 minutes

Ingredients
Prepared pie dough for two 9-inch pie crusts
Egg wash (1 egg mixed with 1 tablespoon water)

Filling
5 cups northwest wild blue huckleberries
1¼ cups white sugar
5 tablespoons cornstarch
4 tablespoons tapioca

1 teaspoon lemon zest
1–2 tablespoons cold butter, diced

Vanilla ice cream, for serving (optional)

Directions
1. Preheat the oven to 350°F.
2. Prepare the pie crust by lightly dusting a surface with flour, then rolling half the pastry out in a thick, round circle of 10–11 inches. Place the crust in a 9-inch pie plate and allow some of the dough to hang over the edge.
3. Mix the filling ingredients (except for the butter) in a large bowl, ensuring that the huckleberries well coated. Pour the mixture into the pie crust and dot the filling with a few dabs of butter.
4. Roll the remaining dough out on a lightly floured surface in a thick, round shape of about 10 inches. Place on the pie. Trim excess dough with a knife and seal the edges together around the pie. Cut away any excess dough. With a fork or knife, create a few holes to let the steam evacuate while baking. Brush the crust lightly with the egg wash.
5. Bake in the oven for 75–90 minutes, until the crust is golden brown.
6. Carefully remove from the oven and allow the pie to cool before serving, as the filling will be piping hot.
7. Serve with a scoop of vanilla ice cream, if desired.

Nutrition Information (1 slice)

Calories 360, Total Fat 17.49g, Saturated Fat 4.27g, Carbs 49.24g,
Fiber 0g, Sugars 25g, Sodium 272mg, Protein 3.97g

Nebraska

Runza

Brought to Nebraska by German settlers, runzas are meat-filled bread pockets made of seasoned ground beef, onion, garlic, sauerkraut, and cabbage wrapped with dough and baked to golden perfection. They make a delicious snack.

Serves: 6–8 - Prep Time: 30 minutes - Cook Time: 3–5 hours

Ingredients
2 tablespoons olive oil
1 medium onion, finely diced
1 garlic clove, minced
1 pound lean ground beef
1 cup of prepared sauerkraut, with the juices
½ small green cabbage, shredded
Salt and pepper
Frozen or fresh bread dough for 2 loafs, thawed if frozen
1 egg

4 tablespoons water
Melted butter (optional)

Directions
1. Place a cast iron Dutch oven or deep pan over medium heat and add the olive oil. Sauté the garlic and onion until fragrant and translucent, about 1–2 minutes.
2. Add the ground beef. Using a wooden spoon, break up any lumps and brown for 4–5 minutes, until it changes color. Season generously with salt and pepper. Drain the beef mixture to remove excess liquids.
3. Add the cabbage and sauerkraut. Stir a few times to combine the ingredients well. Cook on low heat for 2–2½ hours or until the filling has reduced and the cabbage becomes tender. (You can also use a slow cooker and cook on low for 3–4 hours.)
4. Preheat the oven to 400°F and line a baking sheet with parchment paper
5. Take the bread dough and roll it out to about ¼ inch thick. Cut into 4×8 inch rectangles.
6. In a small bowl, mix the egg with the water to make egg wash.
7. Spoon about ½ cup of the ground beef mixture into the center of each runza. Fold the dough pieces over and pinch to seal. Place on the baking sheet, seam side down. Brush the bread pockets lightly with the egg wash.

8. Bake the bread pockets for 20 minutes or until you see that the pastry has risen. Reduce heat to 350°F and bake for another 15–20 minutes until golden brown.
9. If desired, brush each runza lightly with some melted butter as soon as they are out of the oven. Allow to cool slightly before serving.

Nutrition Information
Calories 288, Total Fat 8.8g, Saturated Fat 2.9g, Carbs 34.4g,
Fiber 2.9g, Sugars 5g, Sodium 308.6mg, Protein 18g

Nevada

Las Vegas Prime Rib Dinner

Nevada is known for its spectacular culinary art and variety of cuisines. What most, if not all, menus in Las Vegas have in common is the classic prime rib dinner. With so many possible variations, sides, and combos, it is easy to see why this classic dish has remained at the forefront. This traditional prime rib dinner recipe is one you can master too.

Serves: 6 - Prep Time: 10 minutes - Cook Time: 1 hour 41 minutes

Ingredients
4 stalks of celery, cut in half
5 carrots, cut in half
2 red onions, cut in half
2 tablespoons olive oil
5 pounds prime rib beef roast, bone-in
2 tablespoons kosher salt

1 tablespoon ground black pepper
2 teaspoons garlic powder
6 tablespoons olive oil
1 tablespoon prepared horseradish, plus some more for serving
Baked potatoes, for serving

Directions
1. Preheat the oven to 450°F and place the oven rack in the middle position.
2. In a large roasting pan, lay the vegetables in a single layer and drizzle with a little olive oil.
3. In a small bowl, mix the salt, pepper, horseradish, olive oil, and garlic powder to form a fragrant paste. Combine well.
4. Prepare the prime rib by rinsing and patting dry with paper towels to remove any excess liquid. Spread the horseradish mixture all over the roast. Place the prime rib of beef, fatty side up, on top of the vegetable layers. This will allow the heat to circulate and prevent the beef from sticking to the bottom of the pan.
5. Place the prime rib in the oven and roast for 15 minutes. Reduce the heat to 300°F and roast for another 15–20 minutes per pound until cooked through. The internal temperature is 120°F for rare, 130°F for medium-rare, 140°F for medium, and 150°F for well done .

6. When the prime rib is cooked through, remove it from the oven and spoon the juices over the top. Cover with aluminum foil and let rest.
7. Serve with the vegetables, baked potatoes, and horseradish on the side.

Nutrition Information (10 ounces, not including sides)
Calories 562, Total 48g, Saturated Fat 19g, Carbs 1g, Fiber 0g, Sugars 0g, Sodium 395mg, Protein 30g

New Hampshire

Grape Nuts Ice Cream

This state's flavor of ice cream is none other than grape nuts. If you can't get to New Hampshire this summer to try this iconic ice cream, then try this easy-to-prepare recipe for a delicious grape nut ice cream at home.

Serves: 6–8 - Prep Time: 45 minutes - Cook Time: 6 hours cooling

Ingredients
1 cup whole milk
1½ cups heavy cream, divided
¾ cup white sugar
1 pinch salt
1 (8-ounce) package cream cheese, cubed
5 large egg yolks
1 teaspoon vanilla extract
1 cup Grape-Nuts cereal

Directions
1. In a mixing bowl, combine the cream cheese and 1 cup of heavy cream. Use a hand mixer and mix for 1–2 minutes until smooth. Place the bowl in the fridge or in a bowl of ice to chill.
2. Into a small saucepan, pour the milk, the remaining ½ cup heavy cream, and the salt. Cook over medium

heat until warm but not boiling. Remove from heat and allow to cool. Set aside.
3. To make the custard, separate the eggs and whisk the egg yolks together with the sugar in a clean mixing bowl. Keep whisking until a pale yellow color results, about 1 minute. Then slowly add the warm cream and milk mixture while continuing to whisk.
4. Pour into a saucepan and stir slowly on the lowest heat setting so the mixture doesn't curdle or stick to the bottom of the saucepan. Add in the vanilla. When the custard thickens, remove from heat. Put a strainer over a separate bowl and strain the custard to remove any solid bits.
5. Remove the cream cheese mixture from the fridge or ice bowl and slowly combine it with the custard, stirring slowly until smooth.
6. Refrigerate for a minimum of 3 hours until chilled. Using an ice cream maker, churn the cream and then combine it with the cereal. Mix well so that the cereal is well incorporated into the ice cream. Place in the freezer for at least 3 hours before serving.
7. When serving, remove the ice cream from the freezer and scoop into individual serving bowls or cones.

Nutrition Information (½ cup)
Calories 140, Total Fat 7g, Saturated Fat 4g, Carbs 17g, Fiber 0g, Sugars 13g, Sodium 65mg, Protein 0g

New Jersey

Taylor Ham Sandwich A.K.A. Pork Roll Sandwich

In northern New Jersey, this tasty and unique deli meat is called Taylor Ham, whereas in the south of the state, it's usually referred to as Pork Roll. It comes from Trenton, and has been served in New Jersey for more than 100 years. There are even two festivals devoted to it! If you don't live in New Jersey or neighboring states, you might have to order the ingredients online, but it's so worth it!

Serves: 6 - Prep Time: 10 minutes - Cook Time: 10 minutes

Ingredients:

12 slices boxed Taylor Ham / Pork Roll
6 slices American cheese
6 Kaiser rolls
Lettuce, shredded
Russian or Thousand Island dressing
Cucumber, peeled and thinly sliced
Chips and/or cut vegetable sticks for serving

Directions:
1. Make small incisions on each corner of each pork roll slice so it remains flat when it's fried.
2. Warm a large non-stick pan over medium heat. Add the pork roll slices and fry until golden brown, about 1–2 minutes per side. Work in batches so as not to overcrowd the pan.
3. Place a slice of cheese on 6 of the pork roll slices and cover the pan until the cheese is melted.
4. To assemble the sandwich, spread the bottom of the roll with Russian or Thousand Island dressing. Top with shredded lettuce and cucumber slices. Follow with the first pork roll slice (without the cheese). Top with the cheesed pork roll slice.
5. Close the roll and serve with a side of chips and/or vegetable sticks.

Nutrition Information
Calories 460, Total Fat 32g, Saturated Fat 9g, Carbs 34g, Fiber 1g, Sugars 8g, Sodium 1279mg, Protein 21g

New Mexico

Green Chili

A quintessential New Mexico dish with balanced and earthy flavors, green chili is the state's comfort food. This is a traditional recipe for green chili sauce with roasted New Mexico pepper. It's a perfectly seasoned, hearty and warming dish packed with so much flavor!
Serves: 2 - Prep Time: 10 minutes - Cook Time: 8–10 minutes

Ingredients
1 tablespoon canola oil
½ medium onion, finely diced
2 cloves garlic, minced
2 tablespoons all-purpose flour
¼ teaspoon ground cumin

1 bay leaf
Salt and pepper, to taste
1½ cups chicken stock
1 cup roasted New Mexico green chilies, such as Big Jim Hatch chilies, peeled and chopped (can also use canned or frozen)
¼ teaspoon dried oregano

Directions
1. Place a saucepan over medium heat and warm the oil. Cook the diced onions until they become fragrant and translucent, about 2 minutes. Add the garlic and cook for 1 minute.
2. Slowly add in the flour and stir until it thickens and becomes paste-like.
3. Pour in the stock and add the cumin, bay leaf, peppers and cumin. Season to taste with salt and pepper. Whisk to blend the ingredients together. Bring to a boil and reduce the heat to low. Continue cooking for 3–5 minutes until the green chili reaches the desired consistency.
4. Serve hot, as a side or sauce over your main dish.

Nutrition Information (1 cup)
Calories 160, Total Fat: 8g, Saturated Fat 0g, Carbs 24g, Fiber 8g, Sugars 8g, Sodium 680mg, Protein 8g

New York

Buffalo Chicken Wings

Buffalo, New York, is where this dish reached its legendary status. This is New York's favorite recipe for chicken wings, served as a starter, a main or as part of any Super Bowl spread; it's a win amongst New Yorkers. It yields authentically crispy, deliciously spicy baked chicken wings that are best served traditionally with a side of blue cheese dressing.

Serves: 6–8 - Prep Time: 15 minutes - Cook Time: 40 minutes

Ingredients
18 chicken wings, segmented
4 tablespoons vegetable oil
1 teaspoon salt
¾ cup all-purpose flour
½ cup butter
1½ tablespoons apple cider vinegar
¼ teaspoon cayenne (more if you like it spicier)

¼ teaspoon garlic salt
¼ teaspoon Worcestershire sauce
4 tablespoons hot sauce (more if you like it spicier)

For serving
Celery and carrot sticks
Blue cheese dressing

Directions
1. Preheat the oven to 425°F and line a large baking sheet with parchment paper.
2. In a large bowl, season the chicken wing segments with salt and pour in the oil. Using your hands, mix the wings a few times in the bowl. Add the flour and stir to coat the wings well. Arrange the wings on the baking sheet in a single row. Use a second baking sheet if necessary; wings should not overlap each other.
3. Place in the oven and bake for 40 minutes, turning the wings over after 20 minutes. Wings should be cooked through and golden brown.
4. While the wings are in the oven, prepare the sauce. Place a small saucepan over medium heat and add the butter. When it starts to melt, add the hot sauce, vinegar, cayenne pepper, and garlic salt. Stir a few times to combine the ingredients. When the sauce starts to bubble, remove it from the heat.
5. Place the wings in a large serving bowl. Add the sauce and stir to coat well. All wings should be evenly coated. Place the wings on a serving platter

around a small bowl of blue cheese dip and celery and carrot sticks. Serve immediately.

Nutrition Information (4 pieces)
Calories 410, Total Fat 31g, Saturated Fat 11g, Carbs 9g Fiber 0g, Sugars 0g, Sodium 478mg, Protein 21g

North Carolina

N.C. Pulled Pork Sandwich

North Carolina is well known for its barbecue. It boasts many barbecue festivals and has one of the highest rate of BBQ restaurant per capita. This pulled pork sandwich recipe is typical of the area, basted in barbecue sauce and topped with slaw.

Serves: 10 - Prep Time: 30 minutes - Chilling Time: 2-12 hours - Cook Time: 4-6 hours

Ingredients
5-6 pounds Boston butt pork roast
6 cup hickory wood chips
10 large hamburger buns
Apple juice in a spray bottle
1 medium-sized cabbage, finely shredded
½ cup apple cider vinegar
½ cup ketchup
½ cup sugar

1 teaspoon celery seeds
1 tablespoon red chili pepper flakes
1 teaspoon hot pepper sauce, such as Texas Pete
Kosher salt and freshly ground pepper

Dry rub
2 tablespoons brown sugar
2 tablespoons sweet paprika
2 tablespoon ground black pepper
2 tablespoons sea salt
1 teaspoon onion powder
1 teaspoon garlic powder

Barbecue sauce (yields 1½ cup)
1 cup white vinegar
⅓ cup ketchup
⅓ cup apple juice
2 tablespoons brown sugar
½ tablespoon salt
1-2 teaspoons crushed red chili pepper
1 teaspoon black pepper

Directions
1. To prepare the rub, mix all the ingredients in a mixing bowl, and combine well. Smear the rub all over the pork shoulder, and massage gently. Place the roast in a shallow dish, and cover with plastic wrap. Let it rest in the refrigerator at least 2 hours and up to 12 hours. Let the pork roast rest at room

temperature about 45 minutes before starting to cook it.
2. If you have a smoker, prepare for smoking and have the heat reach 225ºF before cooking the pork. Place the soaked hickory chips in the smoker's box. Make sure the grates are clean and oil them with vegetable oil. Place a dripping pan below where the pork will be cooked to collect dripping juices. When the smoke starts, place the pork butt on the grill. Cook for about 4–6 hours, with the cover down, until the internal temperature reaches 190ºF on a meat thermometer. To keep the pork moist, spray with apple juice every 30 minutes after the first 2 hours of cooking.
3. You can also make this recipe on a regular barbecue. Prepare the charcoal or gas barbecue for indirect heat. Clean and oil the grates. The temperature should be maintained around 225ºF. If your barbecue is equipped with a smoking box, fill it with soaked wooden chips. If not, you can prepare a large double layer foil packet with the soaked wooden chips. Perforate the packet several times to let the smoke out. Place the packet below the grill directly above one of the burners. Place a dripping pan where the pork will be cooked. Start the barbecue on high temperature. When the smoke starts, reduce the temperature to low or 225ºF, and place the pork on the grill over the dripping pan. Cover and cook for 4-6 hours.

4. Check once an hour, and add fresh coals and wood chips as needed.
5. While the pork is cooking, prepare the red slaw. Add cider vinegar, ketchup, sugar, red pepper chili flakes, celery seeds, and hot sauce to a large mixing bowl. Whisk vigorously until the sugar has dissolved. Add the cabbage, and mix well. Season with salt and pepper to taste. Cover with a plastic wrap, and let rest in the refrigerator for at least 1 hour before serving.
6. To prepare the barbecue sauce, also known as the Lexington dip, mix all the ingredients in a sauce pan. Bring to a boil on medium-high heat. Reduce heat to low and let simmer 15 minutes. Remove from heat, and set aside for later use.

Nutrition Information (4 pieces)
Calories 382, Total Fat 11g, Saturated Fat 3g, Carbs 33g
Fiber 2g, Sugars 6g, Sodium 724mg, Protein 28g

North Dakota

Kuchen

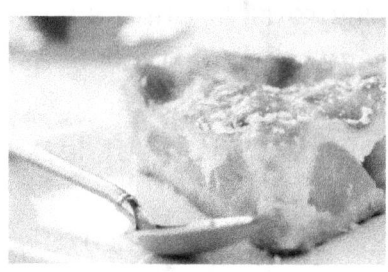

North Dakota serves an authentic recipe that originated with German settlers and has been passed down for generations. Kuchen is an amazingly comforting sweet dough cake, which is filled with fruit and custard.

Serves: 6–8 per pie - Prep Time: 1 hour - Cook Time: 20 minutes

Ingredients
Kuchen base (2 pies)
2 large eggs
1½ cups sugar
1 teaspoon salt
2 cups warm milk
1 (1¼-ounce) package rapid rise yeast
6 cups all-purpose flour
½ cup oil

Vegetable oil for greasing

Fruit custard filling
4 cups heavy cream
6 eggs
1 cup sugar
Dash salt
4 apples, peeled, cored and sliced
2 teaspoons cinnamon
2 tablespoons sugar

Directions
1. To prepare the kuchen pie crusts, whisk the eggs, sugar and salt in a large bowl. Slowly add the warm milk and then mix in the flour and yeast.
2. Grease a clean large bowl generously with vegetable oil. Transfer the dough to this bowl, cover with plastic wrap, and set aside in a warm area so it can rise. It should double in size.
3. Preheat the oven to 350°F and grease a 9-inch baking pan.
4. To make the custard, add the eggs, sugar, heavy cream and salt to a heavy-bottomed saucepan. Whisk over medium heat until the custard thickens. Remove from heat.
5. Prepare the pie crust by lightly dusting a surface with flour and rolling out half the dough into a thick, round circle to fit in a 9-inch deep pie plate. Grease the pie plate with cooking spray. Place the dough in the pie plate. Repeat for the second pie.

6. Arrange the apple slices evenly on top of the dough of each pie.
7. Mix the cinnamon with 2 tablespoons of sugar. Sprinkle evenly over the apples. Pour half of the custard into each kuchen.
8. Place the kuchen in the oven and bake for 20 minutes. Remove from the oven and let cool down for at least 30 minutes before placing in the refrigerator until you are ready to serve.

Nutrition Information (1 slice)
Calories 316, Total 16g, Saturated Fat 10g, Carbs 39g, Fiber 1g, Sugars 22g, Sodium 296mg, Protein 5g

Ohio

Cincinnati Chili

Ohio's favorite chili recipe is loved by locals and visitors alike. A beef chili with a hint of heat, made with onions, cinnamon and cloves, is what sets this chili apart. This great tasting recipe is traditionally served with noodles. Serves: 8 - Prep Time: 8 hours 15 minutes - Cook Time: 3 hours 30 minutes

Ingredients
2 tablespoons olive oil
2 onions, finely chopped
2–3 cloves garlic, minced
2 pounds lean ground beef
4 cups beef stock
2 cups tomato sauce
2 tablespoons apple cider vinegar
2 teaspoons Worcestershire sauce

2¾ tablespoons cocoa powder or 1 ounce grated unsweetened dark chocolate
⅛ cup chili powder
1 teaspoon salt
1 teaspoon cumin
1 teaspoon cinnamon
½ teaspoon cayenne pepper (more if you like it spicier)
¼ teaspoon ground cloves
1 bay leaf
¼ teaspoon ground allspice
Shredded cheddar cheese, for serving
Crackers or crusted bread for serving (optional)
Diced onions (optional)
Noodles for serving (optional)

Directions
1. Place a large saucepan over medium-high heat and heat the olive oil. Sauté the onions and garlic until tender, about 1–2 minutes. Add the ground beef. Using a wooden spoon, break up any lumps and cook until browned. Drain the beef mixture and discard any excess liquid. Return the beef mixture to the pan.
2. Add the beef stock, tomato sauce, apple cider vinegar, Worcestershire sauce, powder, chili powder, salt, cumin, cinnamon, cayenne pepper, cloves, bay leaf, and allspice. Stir a few times to combine the ingredients.
3. Bring the chili to a boil and simmer uncovered on low heat for 1 hour.

4. Top with cheddar cheese and diced onions, if desired. Serve on its own, with crackers or crusted bread, or over noodles.

Nutrition Information (1 cup)
Calories 200, Total Fat 10g, Saturated Fat 4g, Carbs 8g, Fiber 3g, Sugars 3g, Sodium 770mg, Protein 20g

Oklahoma

Chicken Fried Steak

Oklahoma's official meal is the chicken fried steak. If you're not an Okie you might guess that the main ingredient would be chicken, but it's not, beef is! This is a tenderized round beef steak, seasoned, breaded and pan-fried. Topped with a creamy gravy, it will satisfy everyone at your table.

Serves: 2 - Prep time: 10 minutes - Cook Time: 5 minutes

Ingredients
¾ pound round steak
1 large egg
¼ cup milk
1½ cups all-purpose flour
1 tablespoon baking powder
½ teaspoon salt
½ teaspoon freshly ground black pepper

⅛–¼ teaspoon cayenne pepper
½ teaspoon garlic powder
3 cups vegetable or peanut oil for frying

Milk gravy
4 cups whole milk
¼ cup all-purpose flour
1 teaspoon salt
1 teaspoon black pepper

Mashed potatoes and vegetables for serving

Directions
1. Cut the beef in four even pieces. With a meat mallet, pound the steaks between two pieces of plastic wrap or paper until they are ¼ inch thick.
2. In a bowl, whisk the egg and milk.
3. In a shallow dish, mix the flour with the baking powder. Season with the salt, pepper, garlic powder, and cayenne pepper.
4. Dip the steak into the egg mixture and then dredge in the flour mixture, making sure both sides are evenly coated.
5. Place a large cast iron skillet over medium-high heat and warm the oil until it reaches 350°F. Fry the steaks in batches of two until golden brown on each side, 2–3 minutes per side.
6. Place the chicken fried steaks on a plate lined with paper towels to absorb any excess oil.

7. Remove most of the oil from the skillet, keeping the brown bits and about 1 tablespoon of the oil. Place the skillet back on the stove and lower the heat to medium-low. Add all the gravy ingredients and whisk until the sauce thickens, scraping the bottom of the pan to release the flavorful brown bits.
8. Serve the fried steaks with the gravy, your favorite side vegetables, and some mashed potatoes if desired.

Nutrition Information (1 serving)
Calories 496, Total Fat 18g, Saturated Fat 6g, Carbs 68g, Fiber 4g, Sugars 9g, Sodium 1343mg, Protein 19g

Oregon

Hazelnut Squash Soup

Oregon is famous for its hazelnut orchards as well as this favorite dish, an easy-to-make, hearty soup recipe with hazelnuts and squash, perfectly seasoned for cold winter months.

Serves: 4 - Prep time: 10 minutes - Cook Time: 40 minutes

Ingredients
1 (12-ounce) package frozen cooked squash
1 cup Oregon hazelnuts, finely chopped
½ cup finely chopped onion
4 cups chicken broth
Salt and pepper to taste
2 tablespoons butter
2 tablespoons sherry (optional)
¼ teaspoon nutmeg
4 tablespoons heavy cream and hazelnuts for garnish

Directions
1. Place a large saucepan over medium heat and sauté the onions until tender, about 1–2 minutes. Add the broth, squash and hazelnuts and bring to a boil.
2. Add in the remaining ingredients, stir, cover, and simmer for 30 minutes.
3. Use a handheld blender to blend the soup to a nice smooth texture.
4. Place in serving bowls, drizzle 1 tablespoon of heavy cream on top, and decorate with some hazelnuts.

Nutrition Information (1 serving)
Calories 84, Total Fat 1.1g, Saturated Fat 0.6g, Carbs 19.5g,
Fiber 5.9g, Sugars 0.5g, Sodium 485.9mg, Protein 1.6g

Pennsylvania

Philly Cheese Steak

This state's legendary sandwich, the Philly cheese steak, is loved nationwide. It's a thinly sliced steak sandwich, topped with onions and oozy cheese served on hoagie rolls.

Serves: 2–4 - Prep time: 5 minutes - Cook Time: 15 minutes

Ingredients
1 pound ribeye steak, cut in paper-thin slices (see Note below)
1 medium onion, diced
8 slices American cheese
2 long crusty rolls or hoagies
2 tablespoons vegetable oil
Salt and freshly ground black pepper to taste
1 teaspoon garlic powder

4 tablespoons butter, melted

Directions
1. Place a large skillet over medium heat and warm the oil. Sauté the onions until fragrant and translucent. Add the thinly sliced steak and garlic powder. Season with salt and pepper to taste. Cook for a few more minutes until the steak strips are well cooked and tender. Remove from heat and set aside.
2. Slice the rolls lengthwise, but not all the way through. Open and brush with melted butter. Place on a baking tray. Grill under the oven broiler until golden. Line several slices of cheese in each roll and top with the steak-and onion-mixture. Close the sandwich and serve.

Note: To slice the beef at home, a good trick is to place it in the freezer for about 30–40 minutes before slicing against the gain as thin as possible.

Nutrition Information (1 sandwich)
Calories 980, Total Fat 62g, Saturated Fat 23g, Carbs 58g,
Fiber 3g, Sugars 16g, Sodium 1600mg, Protein 41g

Rhode Island

Rhode Island Calamari

Rhode Island's calamari recipe is a starter, side or main so good that locals can't get enough. This is an authentic recipe for pan-fried, breaded calamari which is tossed with a buttery garlic-and-pepper sauce.

Serves: 4 - Prep time: 30 minutes - Cook Time: 20 minutes

Ingredients
1 pound fresh medium-sized squid, cleaned and cut in ½-inch rings, with tentacles
¾ cup corn starch
¾ cup all-purpose flour
½ cup yellow cornmeal
2 teaspoons salt
½ teaspoon freshly ground black pepper
½ teaspoon cayenne pepper

6 cups peanut oil for deep frying
2 cups buttermilk
4 tablespoons unsalted butter
4 garlic cloves, minced
1 cup hot sliced cherry peppers in vinegar, drained
1 tablespoon fresh flat parsley, finely chopped

Directions
1. To a large bowl, add the buttermilk and then the squid rings. Allow them 2–3 minutes to soak in the buttermilk.
2. In a large re-sealable plastic bag, mix the corn starch, cayenne, cornmeal, salt, and pepper. Seal and shake to combine.
3. Preheat the deep fryer to 350°F; or use a large, deep heavy bottomed saucepan: add the oil and warm it on medium to high heat until it reaches 350°F on an instant read thermometer.
4. Take the squid rings from the buttermilk, shake off excess liquid, and place in the dry mix bag. Shake to coat. Work in batches if needed, depending on the size of your bag. Remove squid pieces from bag and shake off the excess flour mixture.
5. Lower them into the fryer (in batches, if necessary to avoid overcrowding) and fry for a few minutes until golden brown. Place the cooked squid rings on a plate lined with paper towels to drain excess oil so they will remain crispy Sprinkle with salt to taste.
6. Place a large frying pan over medium heat and add the butter. Sauté the garlic and hot peppers for 2–3

minutes. Drop the squid rings in and toss to coat evenly for–2 minutes.
7. Place on a serving platter, sprinkle with the chopped parsley and dig in!

Nutrition Information (1 serving)
Calories 421, Total Fat 22g, Saturated Fat 3g, Carbs 30g, Fiber 1g, Sugars 2g, Sodium 689mg, Protein 24g

South Carolina

Shrimp N' Grits

A low country classic, this staple dish is South Carolina's official food. Here's a Charleston-style shrimp and grits recipe, featuring cheesy grits served with shrimp and bacon gravy.

Serves: 4 - Prep time: 15 minutes - Cook Time: 45 minutes

Ingredients
1½ pounds medium shrimp, peeled, deveined, and halved
1 lemon, juiced
Hot sauce to taste
1½ cups stone ground corn grits (not quick-cooking)
1½ teaspoons salt
6 cups water
1–2 tablespoons olive oil
4 slices bacon, diced
1 small onion, finely diced

¼ green bell pepper, finely diced
1 garlic clove, minced
½ cup scallions, finely chopped
2 tablespoons all-purpose flour
1 cup chicken stock
1½ tablespoons unsalted butter
1 cup cheddar cheese, shredded

Directions
1. Put the shrimp in a bowl and add the lemon juice and a few dashes of hot sauce. Stir to coat and set aside.
2. Place a large saucepan over high heat, add the water and salt, and bring to a boil. Gradually add the grits to the boiling water. Stir and reduce heat to low. Cover and let simmer for 35–40 minutes.
3. When the grits are almost cooked, take a large skillet and warm the olive oil over medium heat. Sauté the diced onions for 1–2 minutes, until translucent. Add in the garlic, bacon, green pepper, and scallions and cook for 3–4 minutes. Add the flour and cook for 2–3 minutes. Add in the stock and shrimp and cook until the shrimp are cooked through and change color.
4. When the grits are cooked and they have thickened, add the butter and cheese and stir to combine. Remove from the heat. Add a few dashes of the hot sauce, if desired. Stir a more few times.
5. To serve, scoop the grits evenly into serving bowls and add the shrimp and sauce over the top.

Nutrition Information

Calories 360, Total Fat: 21.2g, Saturated Fat 10.2g, Carbs 21.1g,
Fiber 1g, Sugars 1g, Sodium 1130mg, Protein 23g

South Dakota

Chislic

A distinctive dish of South Dakota which locals are proud to serve as an appetizer is the delicious Chislic. It came to the state with the Germans settlers, and the family recipes have been passed down from the early 1800s. Grilled, seasoned and marinated cubes of meat deliver great flavor as a starter.
Serves: 8–10 (as an appetizer) - Prep time: 10 minutes - Cook Time: 20 minutes

Ingredients
2 pounds mixed meats of lamb, venison, and beef (or use only your favorite)
4 teaspoons Worcestershire sauce
1½ teaspoons salt
½ teaspoon freshly ground black pepper
1 teaspoon garlic powder
1 teaspoon onion powder

2 teaspoons chili powder
Oil for deep frying

Directions
1. Pat the meat with paper towels, trim any excess fat, and cut into bite-size cubes, no larger than ½ inch.
2. To a large bowl, add the cubed meat and the spices. Mix well, cover with plastic wrap, and place in the refrigerator to marinate for 2–3 hours.
3. Prepare short wooden skewers or toothpicks by soaking in cold water for 15–20 minutes.
4. Warm the oil of a deep fryer, or heat oil in a deep heavy bottomed saucepan on the stove over medium-high heat, to a temperature of 350°F.
5. While the oil is warming up, thread 5–6 cubes of meat onto each skewer.
6. When the oil is ready, working in batches, lower the meat skewers into the oil. Let them fry until browned and cooked through, about 2–3 minutes. Place the cooked meat on a plate lined with paper towels.
7. Serve with saltine crackers and a ranch dipping sauce, if desired.

Nutrition Information (1 serving, 4 ounces)
Calories 206, Total Fat 9g, Saturated Fat 3g, Carbs 0g, Fiber 0g, Sugars 7g, Sodium 511mg, Protein 32g

Tennessee

Memphis Sticky Pork Ribs With Corn Hash

Ribs that are fall-off-the-bone tender are the dream of every barbecue chef. A slow grill over low heat paired with classic Memphis barbecue sauce creates the perfect loin rib. Paired with a cool corn hash, this is the perfect Tennessee duo.

Serves: 4–6 - Prep time: 15 minutes - Cook Time: 3½ hours

Ingredients
1–2 pounds pork loin ribs
Classic Memphis BBQ sauce (click here for the recipe)

Corn hash
3 cups fresh whole-kernel corn
1 cup red bell pepper, finely diced
½ cup red onion, finely diced
1 tablespoon vinegar
1 teaspoon sugar
1 tablespoon fresh rosemary
½ teaspoon salt
½ teaspoon pepper

Directions
1. Begin by cleaning and preparing the grill.
2. Bring the ribs to room temperature before grilling, about 30 minutes.
3. Heat the grill to approximately 250°F.
4. Baste the ribs with Memphis BBQ sauce and place on the grill. Cook for 3½ hours, allowing meat to cook slowly and tenderize. Flip and baste the ribs with Memphis BBQ sauce every 30 minutes or so.
5. Combine the corn, bell pepper and onion in a medium sized bowl.
6. In a small bowl, combine the vinegar, sugar, rosemary, salt, and pepper. Add the mixture to the corn and toss, coating thoroughly. Cover and refrigerate.
7. Remove the ribs from the grill and allow them to rest for approximately 10 minutes before cutting and serving.

8. Place a scoop of the corn hash on a plate and top with a portion of saucy loin ribs.

Nutrition Information (4 ribs only)
Calories 360, Total Fat 15g, Saturated Fat 5g, Carbs 4g, Fiber 0g, Sugars 3g, Sodium 469mg, Protein 17g

Texas

Texas Chili

Chili con carne is Texas's official dish, and chili does not, by any proper Texan's definition, have beans in it. Beans are a separate dish all together in this part of the country. Period. This is often called Bowl of Red due to the powerful coloring and flavor provided by the chilies.

Serves: 4–6 - Prep time: 45 minutes - Cook Time: 2 hours

Ingredients:
2½ pounds boneless chuck roast, trimmed and cut into ½-inch cubes
2 ounces dried whole chilies (use Ancho, Guajillo, de Arbol, or a combination)
1½ teaspoons ground cumin
2 teaspoons sea salt

2 teaspoons black pepper
1 teaspoon white pepper
5 tablespoons vegetable oil, divided
3 cloves garlic, minced
⅓ cup diced onion
2 cups beef stock
2 cups water (divided)
2 tablespoons all-purpose flour
1½ tablespoons brown sugar
2 tablespoons apple cider vinegar

For serving
Sour cream
Corn chips
4 ounces cheddar cheese, grated
1 lime, quartered

Directions:
1. Toast the chilies over a flame or medium-high heat for about 3–5 minutes, turning constantly. Do not let them burn. Remove and place in a bowl with hot water. Soak about 30–40 minutes until soft. When softened, split the chilies to remove the seeds. Place in a blender with cumin, salt, black pepper, white pepper and ¼ cup of water. Puree until smooth and set aside.
2. Put 2 tablespoons of vegetable oil in a cast iron pot and heat on medium-high until it begins to smoke. Add the beef in batches, browning 2–3 minutes on each side. Be careful not to overcrowd the pan. Add

more oil if necessary to finish cooking beef. Remove the beef from the pot and set aside.
3. Reduce to medium heat and sauté the garlic and diced onions in the same pot in 1 tablespoon of oil until translucent, about 2 minutes. Stir in the flour and mix well. Add the stock and remaining water and stir to deglaze the pan. Add the chili mixture, beef, brown sugar and apple cider vinegar. Bring to a boil, then reduce to low heat and let simmer for 1½–2 hours until meat is tender.
4. To serve, ladle a helping of chili into a bowl. Top with cheddar cheese, corn chips, sour cream and a lime wedge.

Nutrition Information
Calories 206, Total Fat 9g, Saturated Fat 3g, Carbs 0g, Fiber 0g, Sugars 7g, Sodium 511mg, Protein 32g

Utah

Funeral Potatoes

This traditional potato hot dish was named for its popularity at funerals as a tongue-in-cheek joke among locals, but it's also served as a side with most holiday spreads. A creamy potato casserole, oozy inside with a melted cheese topping, really is perfect for any occasion.

Serves: 4–6 - Prep time: 10 minutes - Cook Time: 55 minutes

Ingredients
4 tablespoons butter
1 small onion, diced
1 32-ounce package frozen shredded hash browns, at room temperature
2 cups shredded sharp cheddar cheese
1 (10.5-ounce) can cream of celery soup
2 cups sour cream

½ teaspoon salt
½ teaspoon black pepper
1½ cups corn flakes cereal, coarsely crushed
½ cup parmesan cheese, grated
Cooking spray

Directions
1. Preheat the oven to 375°F and lightly grease a 9×13-inch baking dish with cooking spray.
2. Place a small skillet over medium heat and add the butter. As it melts, add the onion and sauté for 2–3 minutes until fragrant and translucent. Add in the garlic and stir for 1 more minute.
3. To make the potato mixture, use a large bowl and add the onions, hash browns, cheese, soup, salt and pepper, and sour cream. Mix until all ingredients are well combined.
4. Place the potato mixture in the baking dish and sprinkle the parmesan cheese and the crushed cereal on top.
5. Bake for 45–55 minutes or until golden brown.
6. Allow the potatoes to cool for a few minutes before serving as they will be piping hot.

Nutrition Information (1 serving)
Calories 605.9, Total Fat 34.9g, Saturated Fat 11.7g, Carbs 60.3g,
Fiber 4.7g, Sugars 2.7g, Sodium 1.321mg, Protein 13.3g

Vermont

Vermont Cheddar Cheese Apple Pie

This regional recipe that originates from Vermont is a different take on apple pie. The combination of apples and cheddar cheese makes for a perfectly balanced savory-sweet pie; the cheddar cheese crust is just a bonus.

Serves: 6–8 - Prep time: 40 minutes - Cook Time: 75 minutes

Ingredients
Pie crust
2¼ cups all-purpose flour, plus more for dusting
1 teaspoon sugar
¼ teaspoon salt
1 cup cold unsalted butter, cubed into large chunks

1 cup extra-sharp white Vermont cheddar, grated
4–6 tablespoons cold water

Apple filling
4 Granny Smith apples, peeled, cored, and sliced
4 Gala apples, peeled, cored, and sliced
½ cup granulated sugar
¼ cup all-purpose flour
¼ cup packed light brown sugar
½ teaspoon ground cinnamon
¼ teaspoon freshly grated nutmeg
2 tablespoons cold butter, diced
½ tablespoon lemon juice
Egg wash (beat 1 egg with 1 tablespoon water)
Turbinado sugar, for sprinkling
Vanilla ice cream and Vermont cheddar cheese, for serving

Directions
1. To a food processor, add all the pie crust ingredients except the water. Pulse to mix a few times. Add 4 tablespoons of cold water and continue pulsing until a ball of dough forms. You might have to scrape the sides to make sure all the butter has been mixed with the dry ingredients. If the dough does not hold, add 1–2 tablespoons of water and pulse again. Try not to over-mix, though, as the dough will be tough. Split the dough into two parts and form two flat discs. Cover with plastic wrap and let rest.

2. Preheat the oven to 425°F and place the oven rack in the middle position.
3. To make the apple filling, mix the apples, lemon juice, sugar, cinnamon, nutmeg, flour and salt in a large bowl and stir so that the apples are coated.
4. Prepare the bottom crust of the pie by lightly dusting a surface with flour. Take one disk of dough and roll it out in a round circle larger than the pie plate, about 11–12 inches. Transfer the crust into a 9-inch pie plate and allow some of the dough to hang over the edge for now.
5. Pour the apple filling into the pie crust and spoon in small dots of butter over the filling using a teaspoon.
6. Roll out the remaining dough on a lightly dusted surface in a round shape larger than the pie plate. Transfer the crust to the pie plate atop the filling. Seal both crusts together with your fingers or a fork. Cut away any excess. With a sharp knife, make a few incisions to let the steam escape during baking.
7. Brush the top of the pie lightly with the egg wash and dust with the turbinado sugar. Place in the oven and bake for 20 minutes. Reduce oven temperature to 325°F and bake for another 50–55 minutes, until pie crust is golden brown. Remove pie from oven and let cool down before serving with vanilla ice cream or sliced Vermont cheddar cheese.

Nutrition Information (1 serving)
Calories 330, Total Fat 18g, Saturated Fat 8g, Carbs 40g,

Fiber 3g, Sugars 19g, Sodium 290mg, Protein 10g

Virginia

Virginia Ham Biscuits

Virginians are proud to serve their traditional ham biscuits, and once you try these biscuits, you'll know why. The local country ham is what sets them apart. They're traditional Southern breakfast biscuits which are so good they can be served as a starter or a side too!

Serves: 4–6 - Prep time: 20 minutes - Cook Time: 10 minutes

Ingredients
Dough
1 cup buttermilk
1 teaspoon baking soda
½ teaspoon salt
⅛ teaspoon fresh ground pepper
1 teaspoon baking powder
2 cups all-purpose flour, plus some more for dusting

½ cup plus 2 tablespoons cold unsalted butter

Other ingredients
2 tablespoons melted butter
¼ cup butter, room temperature, for spreading
24 slices Virginia country ham
Mustard (Dijon, prepared mustard or mustard pickle) or pepper jelly, for spreading
12 slices American or cheddar cheese for garnish (optional)

Directions
1. Preheat the oven to 375°F and line a baking sheet with parchment paper.
2. Add all the biscuit dough ingredients to a food processor and pulse until a dough forms. Scrape the side of the processor to make sure all ingredients are well incorporated. Transfer the dough to a floured surface and roll it out into a ½-inch thick rectangle. Make a dozen biscuits with a round, 2½-inch diameter cookie cutter. Brush on both sides with melted butter.
3. Place the biscuits on the lined baking sheet and bake for 8–10 minutes or until golden. A toothpick inserted in the center of a biscuit should come out clean. If not, bake for an additional 1–2 minutes. Remove from the oven and let cool for a few minutes.
4. When the biscuits have cooled, but are still warm, cut them in half. On one half spread butter and on

the other spread the mustard or pepper jelly. Add 2 slices of Virginia ham and 1 slice of cheese, if desired. Close the biscuits and serve.

Nutrition Information (2 biscuits)
Calories 370, Total Fat 19g, Saturated Fat 6g, Carbs 37g, Fiber 1g, Sugars 3g, Sodium 696mg, Protein 15g

Washington

Cedar-Planked Salmon

Only Washington State could cook salmon with such a rich and distinctive taste. This method of cooking will delight you and all the salmon lovers at your table. It produces an earthy, smoky and rich grilled salmon with an added depth of flavor thanks to the cedar planks.
Serves: 2 - Prep time: 15 minutes - Cook Time: 20 minutes

Ingredients
2 tablespoons vegetable oil
1 tablespoon rice vinegar
½ teaspoon sesame oil
2 tablespoons soy sauce
2 green onions, diced, plus some more for garnish
1 teaspoon freshly grated ginger

1 garlic clove, minced
2 salmon fillets, about 8 ounces each, skin removed
½ cup dry white whine
Steamed vegetables and rice
Lemon wedges for garnish

Equipment
12-inch cedar plank, soaked in warm water for at least 1 hour before using

Directions
1. In a small bowl, whisk together the vegetable oil, sesame oil, rice vinegar, soy sauce, green onions, ginger, and garlic.
2. Rinse the salmon fillets and place them in a resealable bag. Pour the marinade over the fillets. Seal the bag and gently massage the fish to distribute the marinade evenly. Refrigerate for 1 hour, turning the fillets over once so both sides are marinated evenly.
3. Preheat a gas barbecue and set the temperature to medium heat. Place the plank on the grill and wait for it to begin smoking.
4. Remove the filets from the bag, preserving as much of the marinade as possible. Place the salmon fillets directly onto the plank and cover loosely with foil. Grill for 15–20 minutes or until the salmon is cooked through.
5. While the fillets are cooking, place the remaining marinade in a small saucepan, add the white wine,

whisk and bring to a boil. Reduce heat to low and let simmer for 5 minutes until the sauce thickens.
6. To serve, drizzle some of the sauce onto the serving plate and lay the salmon on top. Sprinkle with green onions. Serve warm with your favorite sides of steamed vegetables, rice, and lemon wedges.

Nutrition Information (6 ounces)
Calories 241, Total Fat 11g, Saturated Fat 2g, Carbs 0g, Fiber 0g, Sugars 0g, Sodium 75mg, Protein 34g

West Virginia

Pepperoni Rolls

West Virginia's pepperoni rolls are so good they will become a staple snack in your home. Spicy pepperoni enveloped in sweet, fluffy dough, this recipe is the perfect homemade savory treat.

Serves: 20 - Prep time: 2 hours - Cook Time: 16–18 minutes

Ingredients
Dough
1 cup warm water
½ teaspoon white sugar
1 package active dry yeast
2 large eggs
5 cups all-purpose flour
¾ cup white sugar
2 teaspoons salt

½ cup butter, melted

Other ingredients
8 ounces sliced pepperoni
Olive oil
Melted butter for brushing (optional)

Directions
1. Into a small bowl, pour the warm water (temperature should be between 105°F and 115°F), ½ teaspoon of sugar, and the yeast. Stir a few times to dissolve and set aside for 4–6 minutes.
2. To a food processor fitted with a dough hook, add the eggs, ¾ cup sugar, yeast mixture, salt, and add melted butter. Pulse a few times to combine. Gradually add the flour and pulse until a dough ball forms. Set the processor to knead for 30 more seconds. Grease the bottom of a large mixing bowl with olive oil. Add dough and brush lightly with olive oil. Cover with plastic wrap, place somewhere warm, and let rise for about 1 hour, or until doubled in size.
3. Preheat the oven to 350°F and line a baking sheet with parchment paper.
4. Lightly dust a surface with flour, place the dough on the surface, and punch it in the middle. Divide the dough in 20 even parts. Form each roll into a flat 4-inch square. Divide the pepperoni evenly between the rolls. Fold over and pinch the edges to seal.

5. Place the pepperoni rolls on the baking sheet and place in the oven. Bake for 16–18 minutes, until golden brown. Brush lightly with melted butter as soon as you take them out of the oven, if desired. Let rest 10 minutes before serving. Rolls can be served warm or cold.

Nutrition Information (1 serving)
Calories 213, Total Fat 8.8g, Saturated Fat 2.2g, Carbs 25.7g,
Fiber 1.1g, Sugars 3.4g, Sodium 433.5mg, Protein 6.1g

Wisconsin

Wisconsin Bratwursts

Wisconsin's annual Brat Fest proves this state's dedication to its favorite dish. This classic recipe is always featured at Brat Fest, and it always impresses.
Serves: 6 - Prep time: 10 minutes - Cook Time: 40 minutes

Ingredients
2 tablespoons olive oil
1–2 onions, halved and thinly sliced
2 dark beers (12 ounces each)
¼ cup brown sugar
6 bratwursts
2 garlic cloves, minced
1 teaspoon paprika
½ teaspoon caraway seeds
4 cups sauerkraut, drained

For serving
Toasted hotdog buns
Dijon or favorite mustard
Ketchup
Diced onions

Directions
1. Place a large skillet over medium heat and warm the oil. Add the onion and cook until caramelized, about 4–5 minutes. Add the garlic, paprika and caraway, and sauté for 1 minute. Add the beers and brown sugar and bring to a boil. Add the bratwursts and let simmer for 8–10 minutes.
2. In the meantime, prepare your outdoor grill by cleaning and oiling the grate. Set the heat to medium. Remove the bratwursts from the skillet and place them on the grill. Cook until grilled on all sides, just a few minutes. Alternatively, you can also grill the bratwurst in a little olive oil in a grilling skillet over the stovetop.
3. While the bratwursts are grilling, bring the beer mixture to a boil and add the sauerkraut, stirring occasionally. Remove from heat when the bratwursts are ready and the sauerkraut is warm enough.
4. Serve the bratwursts as is with a side of sauerkraut and mustard, or place in toasted hotdog buns with your favorite mustard or ketchup and some sauerkraut.

Nutrition Information (1 bratwurst with sauerkraut)
Calories 344, Total Fat 24.6g, Saturated Fat 8.4g, Carbs 16.6g,
Fiber 2.5g, Sugars 11.1g, Sodium 1222mg, Protein 12.8g

Wyoming

Wyoming Bison Burgers

American buffalo is the meat of choice in this state. Wyoming's bison burgers are so good you only need to try them once to understand why the locals are so proud to serve this dish. Buffalo meat makes a rich, savory and flavorful pan seared burger that's even better when topped with a smoky barbecue sauce and served on a Kaiser roll.

Serves: 4 - Prep time: 10 minutes - Cook Time: 15–20 minutes

Ingredients
1½ pounds ground bison
Salt and pepper, to taste
Garlic powder, to taste
½ tablespoon olive oil
1 tablespoon butter
4 Kaiser rolls
French fries or onion rings for serving

Toppings
4 slices aged cheddar cheese
4 tablespoons mayonnaise
4 lettuce leaves
Sliced butter pickles
½ red onion, sliced
¼ cup sweet barbecue sauce

Directions
1. In a large bowl, mix the ground bison with salt, pepper, and garlic powder to taste. Gently combine with your hands and form 4 patties.
2. Place a large skillet over medium heat and warm the oil and butter. Cook the bison burgers for 3–6 minutes on each side, or until cooked as you prefer.
3. While they are still in the skillet, with 1–2 minutes cooking time remaining, top each one with a cheese slice. Remove from heat when the cheese melts.
4. Turn the oven broiler on and spilt the Kaiser rolls in half. Place under the broiler and lightly toast until warm. Spread the Kaiser rolls with mayonnaise.
5. Layer lettuce and onion slices on the bottom half of the Kaiser rolls. Top with the bison patties with cheese and the butter pickles. Spread some barbecue sauce on the top half of the rolls.
6. Assemble the rolls and serve with a side of French fries or onion rings.

Nutrition Information (1 bison burger and roll)

Calories 435, Total Fat 7g, Saturated Fat 5.9g, Carbs 38g,
Fiber 4g, Sugars 34g, Sodium 382mg, Protein 30g

Washington D.C.

Chili Half Smokes

An iconic dish of Washington D.C. and known to locals as a Chili Dog, this is one original and amazingly delicious recipe which has truly earned its legendary status and following across America.

Serves: 8 - Prep time: 10 minutes - Cook Time: 30 minutes

Ingredients
Chili
2 tablespoons canola oil
¾ pound ground beef
1 yellow onion, diced
3 tablespoons chili powder, divided
1 teaspoon dried mustard powder
Kosher salt and black pepper
½ teaspoon ground coriander
¼ teaspoon ground cumin

1 clove garlic, minced
¼ cup tomato paste
2 tablespoons all-purpose flour
2 tablespoons butter
2 tablespoons apple cider vinegar
2 cups chicken stock

Other ingredients
8 regular half-smoke hot dogs
8 hot dog buns
Diced onions for garnish
Yellow prepared mustard, for spreading

Directions
1. Place a large skillet over medium heat and warm the oil. Add the onion and sauté for 1–2 minutes until tender. Add the ground beef and use a wooden spoon to break up any lumps. Cook until browned. Drain the excess liquid and return the beef and onions to the skillet.
2. Add 1 tablespoon of the chili powder, as well as the mustard powder, salt and pepper to taste, coriander, cumin, and garlic. Mix until incorporated with the beef and onions. Add the tomato paste and cook for 2 minutes, stirring the mixture constantly. Remove from heat.
3. Place a large saucepan over medium heat and melt the butter. Add the flour, stirring quickly for 1–2 minutes. When this has thickened, add in the beef

mixture, the remaining chili powder, vinegar, and the stock.
4. Bring the mixture to a boil and simmer on low heat for 35–40 minutes so that it is reduced and the chili has the desired consistency.
5. Using a grilling pan or panini press on medium-high heat, grill the hotdogs until cooked through and well grilled on all sides, about 2–3 minutes. Set aside.
6. Grill the hot dog buns on both sides. Spread the buns with some prepared mustard and put a half smoke in the center. Layer the chili sauce on top of the half smoke, add some diced onions, and serve.

Nutrition Information (1 dog)
Calories 510, Total Fat 34.4g, Saturated Fat 5.5g, Carbs 36g,
Fiber 9g, Sugars 19.2g, Sodium 940mg, Protein 13.6g

Bonus Recipes

Arroz Con Gandules
(Puerto Rican Rice With Pigeon Peas)

Puerto Rico's traditional dish, which is served at most holiday tables and get-togethers, is one that has to be shared. This classic recipe, which combines rice, peas, and sofrito, delivers a dish so tasty it can be served on any occasion.
Serves: 4 - Prep time: 5 minutes - Cook Time: 25 minutes

Ingredients
1 tablespoon extra-virgin olive oil
⅓ cup sofrito
⅓ cup bacon, finely diced
2 cups white long grain rice
3½ cups chicken stock

1½ teaspoons sazón con achiote y cilantro (coriander and annatto seasoning)
⅓ cup tomato sauce
1 teaspoon dried Italian seasoning
¼ cup fresh cilantro, chopped
2 bay leaves
1 (15-ounce) can pigeon peas, drained and rinsed

Directions
1. Place a Dutch oven over medium heat and warm the olive oil. Add the sofrito and stir until fragrant. Add the bacon, sazón con achiote y cilantro, and tomato sauce. Stir for 4–5 minutes. Add the chicken stock, cilantro, bay leaves, Italian seasoning, and pigeon peas, and bring to a boil.
2. Add the rice to the boiling mixture and stir to combine all the ingredients. Cook uncovered for 15–20 minutes until the water has been reduced. Reduce heat to low and continue cooking, covered, for another 20 minutes. Use a fork to fluff the rice and remove from heat. Remove the bay leaves and serve warm.

Nutrition Information (1 cup)
Calories 241, Total Fat 3g, Saturated Fat 1g, Carbs 41g, Fiber 4g, Sugars 0g, Sodium 282mg, Protein 11g

Classic Memphis Bbq Sauce

This recipe represents the quintessential Memphis barbecue flavor. Both tangy and sweet, balanced by savory spices, this sauce will please a range of palettes.

Yields: about 2 cups - Prep Time: 10 minutes - Cook Time: 30 minutes

Ingredients:
½ cup brown sugar, packed
2 tablespoons molasses
¼ cup apple cider vinegar
1 cup ketchup
½ cup yellow mustard
3 tablespoons Worcestershire sauce
1 teaspoon garlic powder
1 teaspoon onion powder
1 teaspoon celery salt

Directions:

1. Begin by adding the brown sugar, molasses, and apple cider vinegar to a small saucepan. Heat over medium until sugar begins to dissolve.
2. Add the remaining ingredients and increase heat to medium-high. Stir continuously until mixture boils. Make sure all the sugar is dissolved, and the ingredients are well blended.
3. Reduce heat to low, cover and let simmer for approximately 20 minutes. Stir occasionally.
4. Remove sauce from the heat and stir one more time, making sure it's well blended. Set aside and allow to cool slightly before use, or transfer to a covered jar and store in the refrigerator.

Texas Slow Smoked Brisket

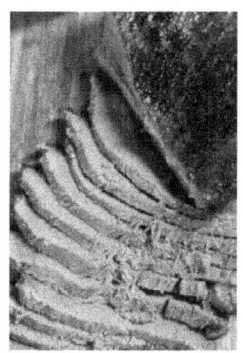

This is one of the foremost foods of Texas. It's just one of the beef dishes that reflect Texas' long history in the cattle industry. This recipe is about the technique, which requires proper equipment and patience. It is well worth the extra effort.

Serves: 8-12 - Prep Time: 15 min. – Chilling Time: 5-12 hours - Cook Time: 3-4 hours 30 min.

Ingredients:
1 brisket, approximately 8–12 pounds
6–8 cups of wood chips (mesquite or pecan is recommended), soaked in water
1 batch brisket dry rub, recipe follows

Sauce Ingredients
1 quart apple juice
1 cup cider vinegar
1 cup barbecue sauce
Combine all ingredients.

Directions:
1. Trim the brisket to ¼ inch of outer fat including the fat near the flat and cap. Sprinkle the brisket with the dry rub and massage into meat. Wrap the brisket in foil and let sit in refrigerator at least 5 hours. Overnight is acceptable.
2. Set up your smoker per manufacturer's instructions. Place wood chips in box and bring smoker up to temperature. Unwrap the meat and place fat side up in the smoker. Brush the sauce on the brisket every hour. The brisket will need about 3–4 hours until internal temperature reaches 165ºF.
3. Remove the brisket from the smoker, brush with sauce and wrap tightly in foil. Continue cooking another 3–4 hours. Final temperature should reach 190ºF. Carefully remove the brisket, retaining all the juices. Allow to rest about 30 minutes prior to slicing.
4. The meat should be thinly sliced across the grain for serving.

Brisket Dry Rub

The dry ingredients of this rub are for a "crust" for a slowly smoked brisket. They add the flavors that permeate the meat in the smoking process. It can be made ahead of time and stored in an airtight container. This recipe will cover a 10–12 pound brisket.

Ingredients:
4 tablespoons paprika
3 tablespoons garlic powder
3 tablespoons celery salt
3 tablespoons mustard powder
2 tablespoons salt

2 teaspoons cayenne pepper
2 tablespoons packed dark brown sugar
2 tablespoons ground cumin
2 tablespoons freshly ground black pepper
2 tablespoons pure chili powder
1 tablespoon dried oregano
1 tablespoon dried basil
1 tablespoon onion powder
1 tablespoon ground white pepper

Directions:
1. Stir all ingredients together until well blended. Store in airtight container.

Conclusion

I hope you have enjoyed this collection of recipes. The amazing combinations of tastes and ingredients differ from state to state, but all of them are full of flavor. Despite the changes a recipe might undergo over time, and the new cooking techniques that have been developed, these classic recipes have stood the test of time and remain at the heart of each state's cuisine.

I have found that locals always follow a simple, straightforward recipe to achieve an authentic dish. That is what's made it possible for these foods to be passed down over the generations, and this regional cultural heritage means we can still enjoy the particular smells and flavors of the authentic dishes served by each state.

Ultimately, this is how a dish is elevated among others. This is how a dish becomes a state icon. And this is how a dish remains a winning classic.

Part 2

American Carrot Cake Recipe

Recipe Servings: 5
Prep Time: 10 Minutes
Cook Time: 01 Minutes
Total Cook Time: 11 Minutes
Difficulty Level: Medium

Ingredients of All American Carrot Cake
- 140 gm brown sugar
- 140 ml oil refined
- 500 gm quark cheese
- 250 gm icing sugar
- 60 gm white butter
- 250 gm carrot
- 150 gm walnut
- 170 gm pineapple
- 3 eggs
- 11 gm cinnamon powder
- 12 gm nutmeg
- 10 gm baking powder
- 10 gm baking soda
- Salt to taste
- 230 gm mascarpone cheese

How to Make All American Carrot Cake
1. Mix together the finely grated carrot, refined oil, castor sugar and brown sugar.

2. In another mixing bowl, mix flour, baking powder, nutmeg powder, cinnamon powder, vanilla essence and eggs.
3. In a different bowl, mix chopped walnuts and chopped pineapple. Keep aside.
4. Mix all of the above and dunk it in a baking dish. Let it bake for 45 min at 180C.
5. After baking, leave it in the oven for 15-20 minutes to rest.
6. Take out the cake and put it in the freezer to chill.
7. In another bowl, mix the quark cheese, mascarpone cheese, white butter and icing sugar and keep aside.
8. Cut the carrot cake in the centre horizontally and fill it with quark cheese and icing sugar.

Apple Pie Recipe

Recipe Servings: 4
Cook Time: 01 Minutes
Total Cook Time: 01 Minutes
Difficulty Level: Easy

Ingredients of Apple Pie
- 125 gms flour
- 100 gms butter(cold)
- 2 Tbsp water
- 1 egg
- 1 apple (peeled and thinly sliced)
- 2 Tbsp of brown sugar
- Pinch of cinnamon powder

How to Make Apple Pie
1. In a bowl lightly knead flour with the cold butter.
2. Add few spoons of water to make the dough compact.
3. Pack the dough in a plastic film and rest for half an hour in the fridge.
4. Place the apples in a bowl. Mix some brown sugar and cinnamon to the apples.
5. Once the dough is set place it between two plastic cling film sheets and roll it out to form a flat round disc.
6. Place the apples in a baking dish.
7. Remove the cling film sheets from the rolled out dough and place it on top of the apples.

8. Make incisions using a fork to the dough for the air to escape.
9. Brush the pastry with whisked egg.
10. Bake the pie at 200°C for 15 minutes, then lower the temperature to 180°C and let it bake for another 20 minutes.

Apple Pie With Raisin Relish Recipe

Recipe Servings: 4
Cook Time: 01 Minutes
Total Cook Time: 01 Minutes
Difficulty Level: Medium

Ingredients of Apple Pie with Raisin Relish
- For apple pie filling:
- 100 gm butter
- 4 medium apple
- 1/3 tsp cinnamon
- 15 -20 gm sugar
- For pie cover:
- 100 gm flour
- 100 gm icing sugar
- 100 gm butter
- 50 ml water
- For raisin chutney:
- 1 Tbsp whole mix spices
- 100 gm raisin
- 30 gm sugar
- 20 ml lemon Juice
- 20 ml orange Juice

How to Make Apple Pie with Raisin Relish
For Apple pie filling:

1. Peel the apples, in a sauce pan, moist the apples with 100 gm of butter and add 1/3 tsp Cinnamon and 15-20 gms sugar, cook it till it becomes thick.
2. Fill the pie shell with the apple mixture.

For Pie cover:
1. Prepare the pie dough, mix 100 gm flour, 100 gm butter, 100 gm icing sugar till it becomes crumbly; add 50 ml water into it to form smooth dough.
2. Divide the dough in two equal pieces. Refrigerate for 1/2 a hr. Roll half of the dough 1/8 inch thick and line the pie pan. Reserve the other half wrapped tightly under refrigeration.
3. Roll out the remaining dough 1/8 inch thick and place it over the filling. Crimp the edges to seal, cutting several vents in the top of the pie. Bake at 180 C, about 45 minutes to 1 hour.
4. Cool to room temperature before serving.

For Raisin chutney:
1. Cook 100 gm raisins, 30 gm sugar, 20 ml lemon juice, 20 ml orange juice and whole spice together on slow fire till it becomes soft.
2. Serve with hot apple pie.

Banana Split Recipe

Recipe Servings: 1
Prep Time: 10 Minutes
Cook Time: 15 Minutes
Total Cook Time: 25 Minutes
Difficulty Level: Medium

Ingredients of Banana Split
- 1 Square Chocolate - semi-sweet
- 2 Tbsp Light Corn Syrup
- 2 Tbsp Condensed Milk
- 1/8 tsp Vanilla Essence
- 1 Tbsp Peanuts (unsalted), roasted
- 1 Small Banana (quartered0

How to Make Banana Split
1. Micro-cook the chocolate on Hi for 2 minutes, stirring once.
2. Also stir in corn syrup and sweetened condensed milk.
3. Micro-cook again uncovered on Hi for 30-45 seconds.
4. Stir in vanilla.
5. Serve warm atop ice cream and sprinkle some peanuts. Arrange the quartered banana around ice cream.

(A banana split is an ice cream dessert with the goodness of bananas. Warm sauce made out of condensed milk and chocolate drizzled over the bananas and ice cream. It is served in a long dish called a boat.)

Blueberry Pancake Recipe

Recipe Servings: 4
Cook Time: 25 Minutes
Total Cook Time: 25 Minutes
Difficulty Level: Easy

Ingredients of Blueberry Pancake
- 6 Tbsp soya flour
- 3 Tbsp soya milk
- 1 egg
- 1/2 tsp baking powder
- 2 tsp sugar substitute
- 3-4 drops maple extract or vanilla essence
- Water
- Canned blueberry

How to Make Blueberry Pancake
1. Whisk together soya flour, soya milk, baking powder, sugar substitute and one egg yolk to make a batter of dropping consistency. Keep aside for 15 minutes.
2. Whip the egg white until fluffy. Fold into the batter.
3. For the maple syrup, heat some water, maple extract and sugar substitute over a medium flame.
4. Heat a pan, spray some olive oil and spoon the batter to make a pancake.
5. Once the underside is half done, sprinkle the blueberries on top and flip.

6. Serve hot sprinkled with sugar substitute or with the maple syrup.

Ceviche Recipe

Recipe Servings: 3
Prep Time: 05 Minutes
Cook Time: 30 Minutes
Total Cook Time: 35 Minutes
Difficulty Level: Medium

Ingredients of Ceviche
- 1 kg fish fillet - small pieces
- 2 cups lemon juice
- 2 Tbsp olive oil
- 3 garlic cloves
- 1 kg tomato - diced
- 1 cup onions - chopped
- 3 Tbsp coriander - chopped
- 3 Tbsp ketchup
- 2 tsp tobasco sauce
  - Salt
- Black pepper
- 1/2 cup jalapeno peppers - chopped
- 1 cup olives - chopped

How to Make Ceviche
1. Marinate the fish in lemon juice and leave for about 3 hours.
2. Heat olive oil in a pan and saute garlic till golden brown. Keep aside.

3. Take a bowl and mix all the other ingredients with the fish.
4. Season with salt and pepper.
5. Remove the garlic from olive oil and add it to the fish. Mix well.
6. Garnish with olives and serve.

Chicken And Fish 65 Burgers Recipe

Prep Time: 10 Minutes
Cook Time: 30 Minutes
Total Cook Time: 40 Minutes
Difficulty Level: Easy

Ingredients of Chicken and Fish 65 Burgers
- 2 Tbsp ginger-garlic paste
- 3 tsp red chili powder
- 1 1/2 tsp turmeric powder
- 2 tsp coriander powder
- Handful curry leaves
- 5 Tbsp refined oil
- Salt to taste
- 100 gm chicken breast
- 200 gm fish fillet
- 200 gm rice flour to coat
- 2 Tbsp mayonnaise
- 3 tsp tomato ketchup
- 1/2 tsp Tabasco
- 3 burger buns
- 1 onion
- 3 tomatoes

How to Make Chicken and Fish 65 Burgers
1. In a bowl add the ginger-garlic paste, chili powder, turmeric powder, a tsp of coriander powder & some chopped curry leaves.

2. Season it with some salt and drizzle a Tbsp of refined oil to bring it all together.
3. Trim the chicken breast and cut the fish fillet.
4. Add marinate on each piece, making sure that the pieces are nicely coated with the masala.
5. In a non-stick pan, add refined oil and let it heat up.
6. Roll the chicken and fish pieces in rice flour till they are fully coated & shallow fry the coated chicken and fish in the non-stick pan.
7. Take the burger buns and slit open from the center.
8. Spread the burger sauce over half of the burger bun halves.
9. Add the chicken breast on one half and fish pieces on the other.
10. Then add tomatoes and onion slices and lettuce on each of them.
11. Sprinkle some pepper to taste and cover both chicken and fish with the other half bun halves.

For the burger sauce:
1. In a bowl, add mayonnaise, tomato ketchup and some Tabasco sauce for a tangy taste.
2. Then add coriander powder and chili powder.
3. Whisk it all together.
4. Serve the burgers with a light apple salad.

(Delight your taste buds with this burger recipe. A burger made with chicken, fish fillets, tomatoes and a tangy hot and sour sauce.)

Chilli Burgers With Pepper Relish Recipe

Recipe Servings: 5
Prep Time: 10 Minutes
Cook Time: 30 Minutes
Total Cook Time: 40 Minutes
Difficulty Level: Easy

Ingredients of Chilli Burgers with Pepper Relish
- 50 gm butter
- 2 large diced onions
- 3 chopped red chillies
- 2 tsp cumin roasted, ground
- 400 gm lamb, minced
- 1 Tbsp mustard
- 1 Tbsp Worcestershire sauce
- 300 gm kidney beans, pureed, cooked
- 75 gm fresh bread crumbs
- 4 Tbsp parsley, chopped
- 1 large egg, beaten
- Oil for shallow frying
- 6 buns
- 1 onion, sliced
- 2 large tomatoes, sliced
- 1 lettuce, shredded
- Flour to coat
- For roasted pepper relish:
- 1/2 kg red bell peppers, quartered and seeded

- 1 tsp roasted cumin
- 2 Tbsp chilli sauce, mild and sweet
- 50 ml salad/olive oil

How to Make Chilli Burgers with Pepper Relish
1. For the relish:
2. Grill peppers until skin blackens. Remove skin.
3. Blend the peppers with cumin and sauce until smooth.
4. Gradually add oil.
5. Cover and chill before using.

For the chilli burger:
1. Heat butter, add onion, chillies and cumin.
2. Cook until onion softens.
3. Combine with meat, mustard, sauce, bean paste, breadcrumbs, parsley and egg. Mix well. Shape into 6 large patties.
4. Chill well and coat with flour. Shallow fry in hot oil until colored and cooked.
5. Halve and toast bread rolls. Spread with relish, top with burgers, lettuce, onion rings and tomato slices.

(An American recipe of chilli burgers. A spiced lamb patty slapped between burger buns served with a roasted red bell pepper dip.)

Classic American Pancakes Recipe

Recipe Servings: 2
Prep Time: 05 Minutes
Cook Time: 25 Minutes
Total Cook Time: 30 Minutes
Difficulty Level: Easy

Ingredients of Classic American Pancakes
- 1 cup all-purpose flour
- 2 1/2 tsp baking powder
- 1/2 tsp salt
- 3/4 Tbsp white sugar
- 3/4 cups milk
- 1 small egg
- 2 Tbsp butter, melted
    - Toppings
- Melted butter
- Maple syrup or honey
- Mixed berries (or any other mixed fruit of your choice)
- Powdered sugar

How to Make Classic American Pancakes
1. In a large bowl, bring together all the dry ingredients. Make a well in the center and pour in the milk, egg and melted butter. Mix until smooth batter is formed.

2. Heat a lightly oiled frying pan over medium high heat. Pour the batter onto the pan, using approximately 1/4 cup for each pancake.
3. Brown on both sides and stack 2-3 pieces on a plate.
4. Sprinkle with some dusted sugar and top with some whole mixed berries. Serve melted butter and maple syrup on the side.

(Start your day with these classic American pancakes. They are easy to make and can have various toppings like maple syrup or honey or fresh berries- the choice is yours!)

Doughnuts Recipe

Recipe Servings: 20
Prep Time: 05 Minutes
Cook Time: 35 Minutes
Total Cook Time: 40 Minutes
Difficulty Level: Medium

Ingredients of Doughnuts
- 3 1/2 cups maida
- 1 tsp salt
- 5 tsp baking powder
- 1 tsp cinnamon - powdered
- 1 tsp nutmeg - powdered
- 2 Tbsp butter
- 3 cups sugar
- 2 eggs - beaten well
- 3 cups milk
- Oil to deep fry

How to Make Doughnuts
1. Sift maida with salt, baking powder, cinnamon and nutmeg and keep aside.
2. Cream butter and sugar. Add eggs and beat well.
3. Add milk and maida and mix into a dough like consistency.
4. Roll the dough on a lightly floured surface to 1 inch thickness.

5. Cut with floured doughnut cutter and let stand for 15 minutes.
6. Heat oil and add the doughnuts to it over high heat.
7. Turn immediately and lower heat to medium and fry till brown.
8. Drain on absorbent paper and serve.

Ham Rolls Recipe

Recipe Servings: 8
Prep Time: 15 Minutes
Cook Time: 25 Minutes
Total Cook Time: 40 Minutes
Difficulty Level: Easy

Ingredients of Ham Rolls
- 8 slices ham, thinly sliced
- 4 Tbsp (60 gm) cream cheese
- 1/2 cup (100 gm) onion, finely chopped
- 1 Tbsp (15 gm) pickled gherkins , finely chopped
- 4 lettuce leaves, crisped 4
- 1 tsp salt or to taste
- 1/8 tsp black pepper (kali mirch), freshly powdered
- 2 Tbsp (30 gm) mayonnaise sauce
- Some greens for garnish (celery, spring onions, parsley, etc.)

How to Make Ham Rolls
1. Mix the cream cheese, onions, gherkins, mayonnaise, salt and pepper.
2. Divide the mixture into 8 and place a portion each in the center of each slice of ham.
3. Roll like a tube, as tightly as possible, without breaking the ham.

4. Line a serving dish with the lettuce leaves, and arrange the ham rolls over it, keeping the edges down. Garnish with the greens and serve.
5. If making ahead of time keep covered in the refrigerator, to avoid the ham drying up.
6. For vegetarians, substitute blanched and cooled cabbage leaves for ham.

Juicy Lamb Burger Recipe

Recipe Servings: 2
Prep Time: 20 Minutes
Cook Time: 40 Minutes
Total Cook Time: 01 Hour
Difficulty Level: Easy

Ingredients of Juicy Lamb Burger
- 1/2 kg lamb keema
- 1 egg
- 1 Tbsp rosemary leaves
- 1/2 Tbsp red rice flakes
- 1 Tbsp garlic
- 1 Tbsp salt
- 1/2 Tbsp black pepper
    - Oil
- 2 burger buns
- Lettuce
- 4 sliced tomatoes

How to Make Juicy Lamb Burger
1. First start with 1/2 kg of lamb keema. Then add of one egg, some rosemary leaves and rice flakes.
2. Put 1 tsp garlic paste, salt and 1/2 tsp black pepper. Now mix it all well by hand.
3. In a pan add some oil.
4. Make 2 small rounds of keema paste, then fry it from the both side, then take 2 sliced

5. burger and fry it in the pan.
6. Now keep the sliced bun on the plate and put lettuce, sliced tomatoes, onion, and fried keema patties on the burger.
7. Cover it with a second bun and your lamb burgers are ready.

Kfc Style Fried Chicken Recipe

Recipe Servings: 4
Prep Time: 15 Minutes
Cook Time: 30 Minutes
Total Cook Time: 45 Minutes
Difficulty Level: Easy

Ingredients of KFC Style Fried Chicken
- 8 chicken drumsticks/breast
- 100 ml curd
- 1 beaten egg
- 50 gm all purpose flour
- 50 gm bread crumbs
- 1 tsp chilli powder
- 1 tsp white pepper powder
- 1 tsp onion, dried and powdered
- 1 tsp basil/tulsi leaves, dried and powdered
- 1 tsp oregano / omam leaves, dried and powdered
- 1 green chilli, chopped
- 1 tsp garlic, dried and powdered
- 1 tsp ginger, dried and powdered
- Salt to taste
- Oil for frying

How to Make KFC Style Fried Chicken
1. Wash and clean chicken. Drain water well from chicken.

2. Add beaten egg, curd, 1/2 tsp chilli powder, salt to chicken and mix well. Marinate it for at least 3 to 4 hours.
3. Mix all purpose flour, green chillies, white pepper, oregano, garlic, ginger, basil or tulsi leaves, remaining chilli powder and salt.
4. Cover marinated chicken with spicy all purpose flour mix and then with bread crumbs.
5. Heat oil in a thick bottom kadai and deep fry the chicken in a slow fire till it is cooked.
6. Serve hot with tomato ketchup.

Lamb And Pork Burger With Chunky Salad Recipe

Recipe Servings: 2
Prep Time: 10 Minutes
Cook Time: 01 Hour
Total Cook Time: 01 Hour 10 Minutes
Difficulty Level: Medium

Ingredients of Lamb and Pork Burger with Chunky Salad
- For lamb and pork burger:
- 250 grams minced pork
- 250 grams minced lamb
- 8-10 cream crackers
- 1 Tbsp worcestershire sauce
- 2 onions
- Parsley, finely chopped
- Dijon mustard
- Salt
- Pepper
- Cheese slices
- Burger buns
- 6 slices of bacon
- 1 red chilli, sliced
- 1 egg
- Butter
- Ketchup
- Olive Oil

- For chunky salad:
- 1 cucumber, sliced
- 2 tomatoes, chopped
- 1 yellow capsicum, deseeded and chopped
- 1 red capsicum, deseeded and chopped
- For lemon olive oil dressing:
- Extra virgin olive oil
- Juice of 1 lemon
- Sea salt
- Pepper

How to Make Lamb and Pork Burger with Chunky Salad

For lamb and pork burger:
1. Put the crackers in a zip-lock bag and pound until crushed.
2. In a large mixing bowl, add the crackers, parsley, one finely sliced onion, red chilli, one teaspoon of mustard, egg and Worcestershire sauce to minced pork and lamb and mix well. Season to taste.
3. Roll the mixture into patties and cook them for 3-4 minutes on each side in a griddle pan.
4. In another pan, heat bacon till crisp. Remove bacon from the pan and add thickly sliced onion to the excess bacon fat left in the pan.
5. Add a bit of butter, some ketchup, mustard and olive oil to it. Fry the onions till translucent.
6. Finally, toast the buns and layer them with the onion mixture, fried bacon, the patty and finish off with a cheese slice.

7. To Serve: Serve with chunky salad and fries on the side.

For chunky salad with lemon olive oil dressing:
1. In a bowl, whisk the extra virgin olive oil, lemon juice, salt and pepper to make the dressing.
2. Chop the vegetables .
3. Add some dressing to the chopped vegetables and toss .
4. To Serve: Serve with Burger and fries on the side.

Lamb Burger With Radish Slaw Recipe

Recipe Servings: 1
Prep Time: 10 Minutes
Cook Time: 30 Minutes
Total Cook Time: 40 Minutes
Difficulty Level: Easy

Ingredients of Lamb Burger with Radish Slaw
- For the burger:
- 500 gms lamb leg (minced)
- 2 tsp butter
- 1 onion (chopped)
- 3 cloves garlic (chopped)
- 1/3 cup parsley (chopped)
- 1 tsp rosemary (chopped)
- 1 egg yolk
- Salt to taste
- Black pepper to taste
- 1 tsp thyme
- 1/3 cup parmesan cheese
- For the radish slaw:
- 1 mediun white radish (julienne) 1 medium
- 1 tsp parsley (chopped) 1 tsp
- 1/2 cup green apple (julienne) 1/2 cup
- 1 stalk spring onion 1 stalk
- 1/2 lemon juice 1/2 lemon
- A pinch of sugar (a pinch)
- Olive oil and salt to taste

- Pepper to taste
- For green chilli aioli:
- 1 green chilli
- 1 cup coriander
- 1/2 cup mint leaves
- 1 cup mayonnaise
- Salt to taste
- Sugar to taste
- 1/3 cup coconut milk
- 1 tsp balsamic vinegar

How to Make Lamb Burger with Radish Slaw
For lamb burger:
1. In a bowl take lamb mince, break in an egg, grate some parmesan cheese, rosemary and thyme.
2. In a processor blend some onions and garlic.
3. Saute the onions and garlic in some butter on a pan.
4. Add all the contents to lamb mince and mix well. Keep in the fridge.

For Green chilli aioli:
1. Blend all the ingredients.

For the radish slaw:
2. In a stainless steel bowl, mix all and toss well.

Lentil-Mushroom Burgers Recipe

Recipe Servings: 4
Cook Time: 01 Hour
Total Cook Time: 01 Hour
Difficulty Level: Medium

Ingredients of Lentil-Mushroom Burgers
- 5 whole-wheat hamburger buns
- 2-3 Tbsp olive oil
- 1 medium onion, diced small
- 3 cloves of garlic, minced
- 1 package cremini or button mushrooms, minced
- 4 sun-dried tomatoes, chopped fine
- 1 cup cooked brown lentils
- 1/2 an egg
    - Salt
- Pinch of black pepper
- Pinch of white pepper
- 1 blob of butter with 2-3 cloves minced garlic (for buns)
- Caramelized onions
- 5 lettuce leaves
- 5 slices of tomatoes

How to Make Lentil-Mushroom Burgers
1. Process 1 burger bun in a food processor to make crumbs. Set aside.

2. In a saute pan, heat the olive oil over medium-high and saute onions with a pinch of salt until soft.
3. Add the garlic, stir, and cook another minute.
4. Scrape the onion mix into a bowl. Keep aside.
5. Add another tablespoon of olive oil to the pan, over high heat, add the mushrooms followed by salt - let the mushrooms sweat.
6. Reduce the heat to medium and continue to cook until the liquid evaporates and the mushrooms turn deep golden brown.
7. Scrape the mushroom mixture into the bowl with the onions-set aside to cool for a couple of minutes.
8. Meanwhile heat some butter with garlic and toast the buns lightly.
9. Now in the food processor add the sun-dried tomatoes, the lentils and half of the mushroom-onion mix, process so that it is pasty yet have a bite. Pulse it slightly, do not puree.
10. Put the mixture into a mixing bowl and mix in the egg, a pinch of salt, black and white pepper.
11. Divide the lentil mixture into four portions, make each into a ball and flatten into a patty.
12. Coat the patty with the breadcrumbs.
13. Heat oil in a pan. Add the lentil patties and shallow fry on each side until crisp and deep golden.
14. Now bake the patties for 5-6 minutes at 180 degree Celsius.
15. We put it in the oven because the patties were shallow fried i.e the outside gets cooked but the inside is still mushy.

16. Place a lettuce leaf, tomato slice and some caramelized onions on each of the buns.
17. Top with the patty and close with the other half.

(Now burgers that are healthy. Patties made with mushrooms, lentils and sun-dried tomatoes sliced between whole wheat buns.)

Meat Loaf Recipe

Prep Time
Cook Time: 01 Hour
Total Cook Time: 01 Hour
Difficulty Level: Medium

Ingredients of Meat Loaf
- 740 gm minced meat
- 100 gm fresh breadcrumbs
- 4 Tbsp lemon juice
- 2 tsp garlic paste
- 3 ground onions
- 2 tsp dried basil
- Salt and pepper
- 1 beaten egg
- 1 Tbsp beaten butter
- For the Topping:
- 5 Tbsp tomato ketchup
- 2 Tbsp grated jaggery
- 2 tsp prepared mustard
- 2 Tbsp vinegar
- 1/4 tsp mild chilli powder
- 2 cloves
- 1 tsp strained ginger juice
- 1 sliced lime
- For the Rice Salad:
- 8 Tbsp cooked rice
- 1 green capsicum

- 100 gm blanched beans
- 100 gm cooked peas
- 100 gm torn spinach leaves
- 100 gm sliced spring onions
- 2 Tbsp shredded garden herbs
- For the Dressing:
- 4 Tbsp olive/salad oil
- 2 Tbsp lemon juice
- 1 tsp garlic paste
- 1/2 tsp oregano
- Pinch of mustard powder
- Salt and pepper

How to Make Meat Loaf
1. Mix all meat loaf ingredients together.
2. Press into an oiled 1 kg loaf tin.
3. Bake at 180 degrees c for 15 minutes.
4. Mix topping ingredients together. Spoon over loaf.
5. Arrange lemon slices on top. Continue cooking for a further half hour.
6. Serve with rice salad.
7. For Rice Salad:
8. Combine salad ingredients together.
9. Whisk together items for dressing.
10. Pour over rice salad. Chill and serve with meat loaf.

Potato Corn Burgers Recipe

Recipe Servings: 4
Prep Time: 20 Minutes
Cook Time: 35 Minutes
Total Cook Time: 55 Minutes
Difficulty Level: Medium

Ingredients of Potato Corn Burgers
- 4 Tbsp olive oil
- 1/2 a leek
- 1/3 cup chopped celery
- 1/2 chopped onion
- 1 cup corn kernels frozen
- Few sprigs thyme
- Few coriander leaves
- 2 large potatoes roasted and peeled
- 5-6 pieces pickled jalapenos
- 1 tsp garlic chives chopped
- 75 gm feta cheese
- 1 Tbsp corn flour
- 2 Tbsp milk
- 1 cup bread crumbs
- 4-5 Tbsp oil for frying
- 1 tomato
- 1 lettuce leaf
- Few gherkins
- 3-4 tomatoes

How to Make Potato Corn Burgers
1. Heat up 2 tbsp of olive oil in a hot pan; add the onions, leeks, celery and the corn and season with salt and thyme and sauté for 5 minutes
2. Peel the cooked potatoes, grate or mash the potatoes in a bowl.
3. Mix the potatoes with the corn, onion, leeks, celery.
4. Add the jalapenos, a large handful of coriander and crumble the feta cheese into the mixture.
5. Mix all the ingredients really well and season to taste.
6. Let the mixture rest in the fridge for a few minutes.
7. Mix some corn flour and milk to make a light batter.
8. Put the bread crumbs in a plate.
9. Shape the burger patties into with a cutter or mould.
10. Dip the patty in the batter and cover with breadcrumbs.
11. Heat up 2 tbsp oil in pan and shallow fry until nice and brown.
12. Slice up some tomatoes and put it in a lettuce leaf for the garnish along with some gherkins.
13. Heat the buns in the oven.
14. Put the lettuce, tomatoes and gherkins inside the bun along with the patty and serve with
15. chips on the side.

www.ingramcontent.com/pod-product-compliance
Lightning Source LLC
Chambersburg PA
CBHW071830080526
44589CB00012B/972